Unit 1

Look and match.

wave | stand up | clap | point | dance | sit down

New words

Vocabulary: *dance, clap, point, sit down, stand up, wave*

Match and color.

robot

Daisy

Mouse

Robin

Look and draw yourself. Say *Let's dance.*

dance

clap

point

sit down

stand up

wave

Look and match.

jump
climb
stretch
run
strong

Smart topic **Move your body**
Structure: *We're strong!* **Vocabulary:** *run, jump, stretch, climb*

Count and match.

1

2

3

4

5

6

Can you do the action? Trace the ✔ or ✘.

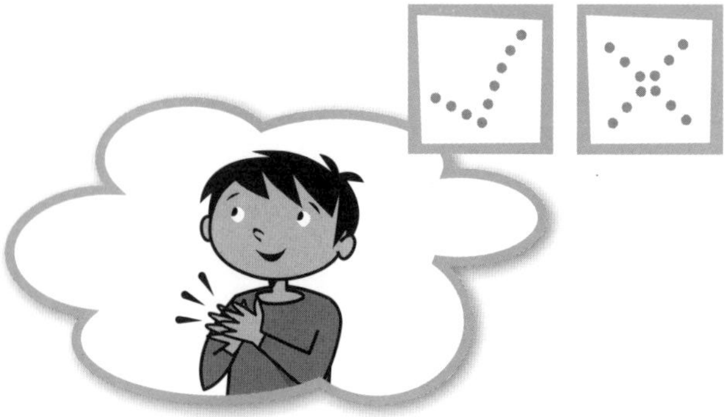

clap

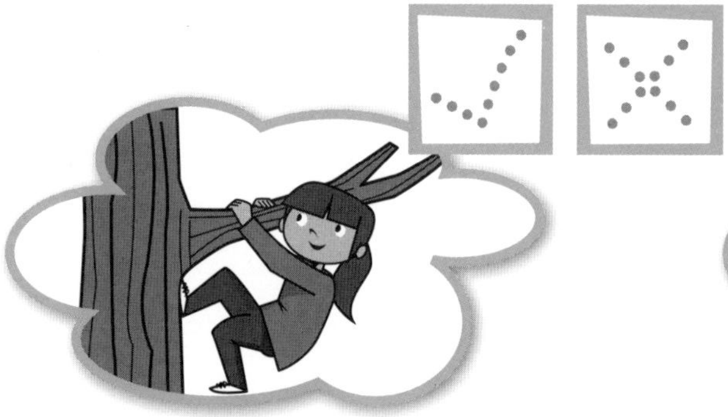

climb

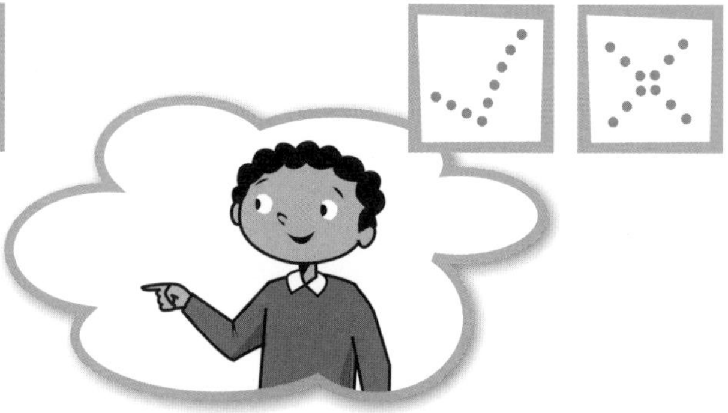

point

stretch

run

wave

jump

dance

Look and draw.

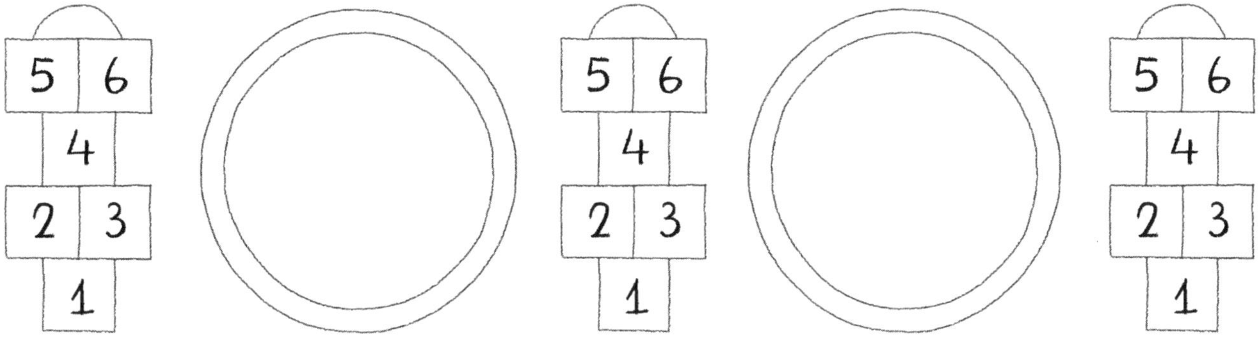
5 6
4
2 3
1
5 6
4
2 3
1
5 6
4
2 3
1

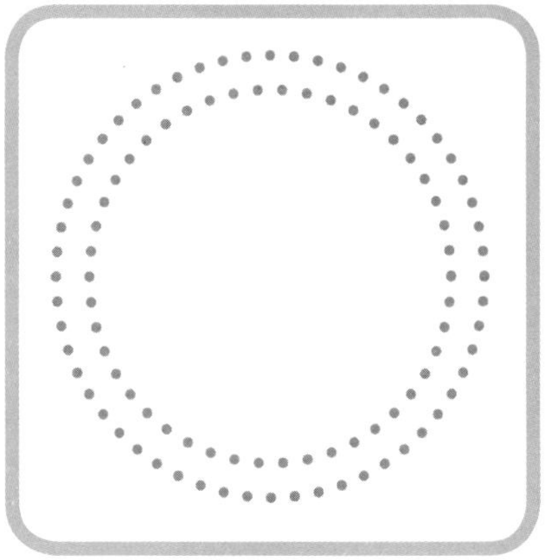

hopscotch hoop

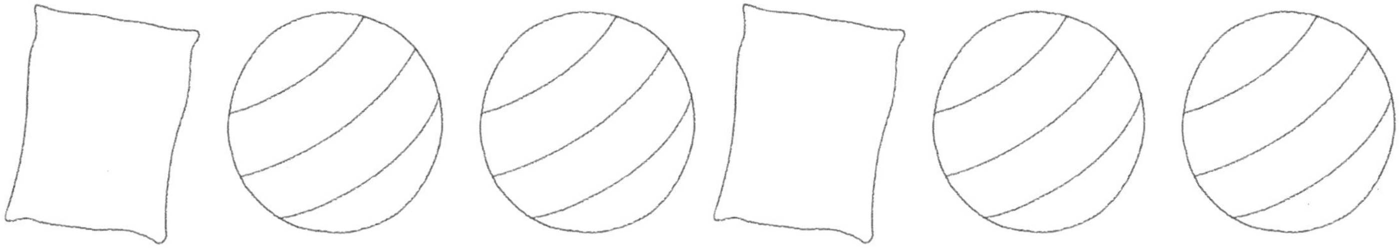

beanbag ball

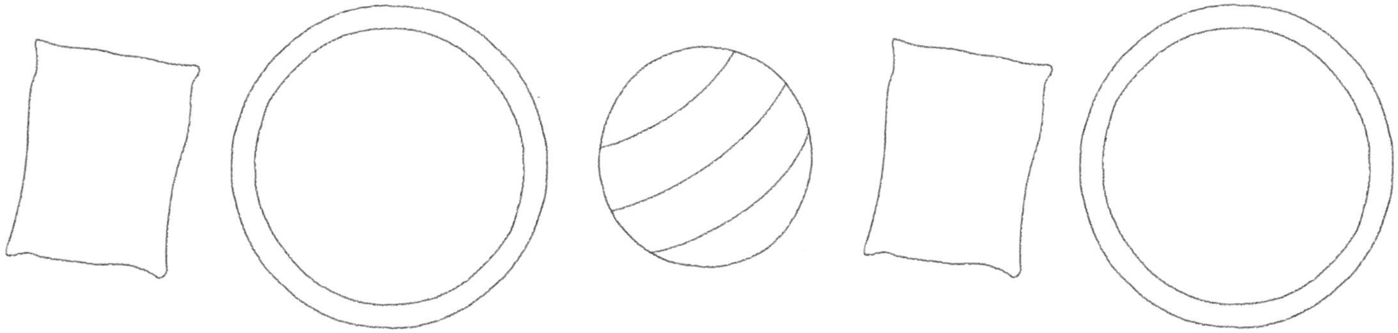

Look and trace.

Let's …

1

roll a hoop

2

dance

3

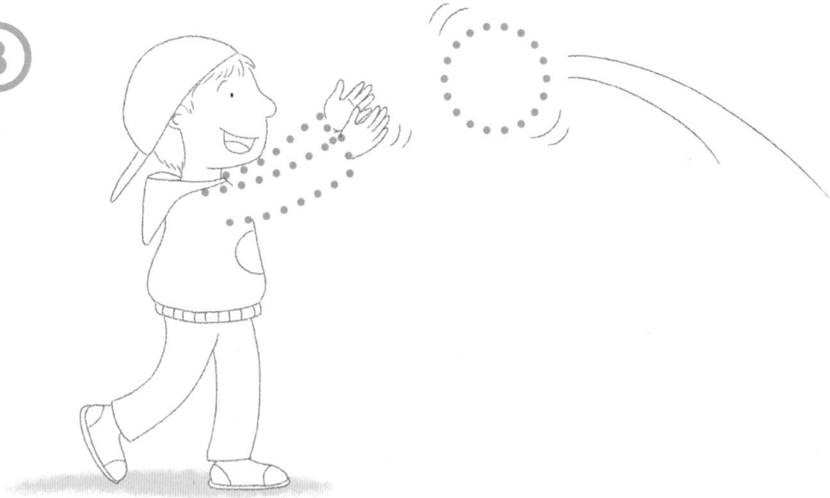

catch a ball

4

throw a beanbag

Literacy Print awareness
Structure: *Let's …*

Follow numbers 1–8.

1
2
3
5
4
5
7
5
6
8
6
7
3
1
8

Trace and match.

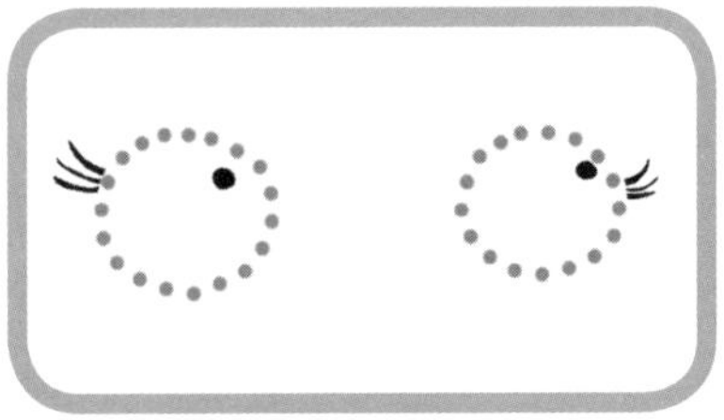

eyes

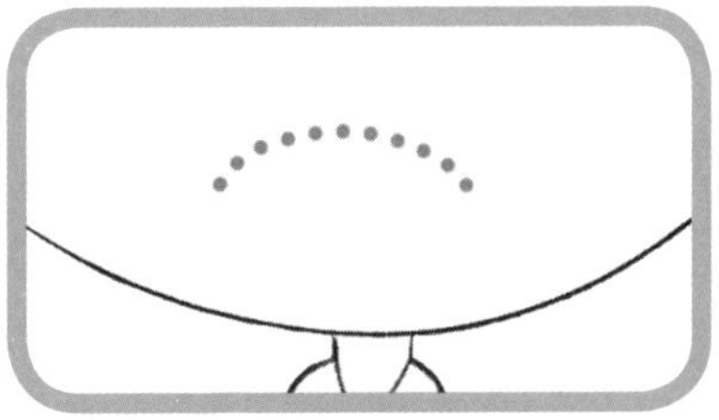

mouth

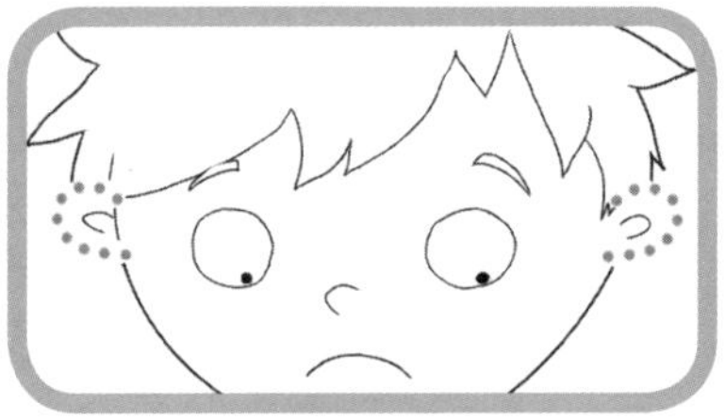

ears

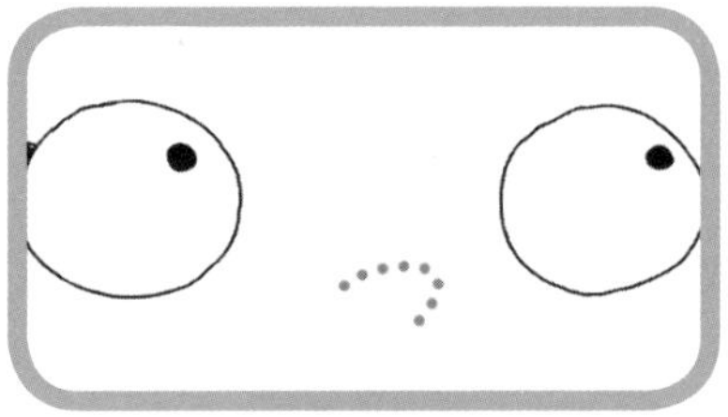

nose

sad
happy

New words
Vocabulary: *ears, nose, eyes, mouth, sad, happy*

Find the monster. Color the circles (◯).

Look and trace. Say *It has 2 eyes. It's sad/happy.*

2 eyes

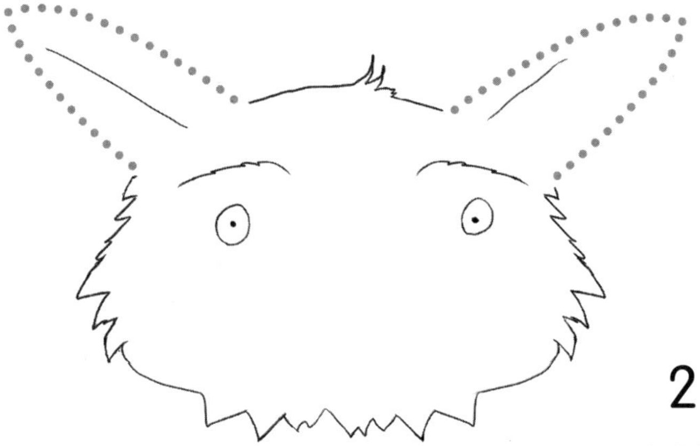

2 ears

1 nose

1 mouth

sad

happy

Look and draw.

dirty

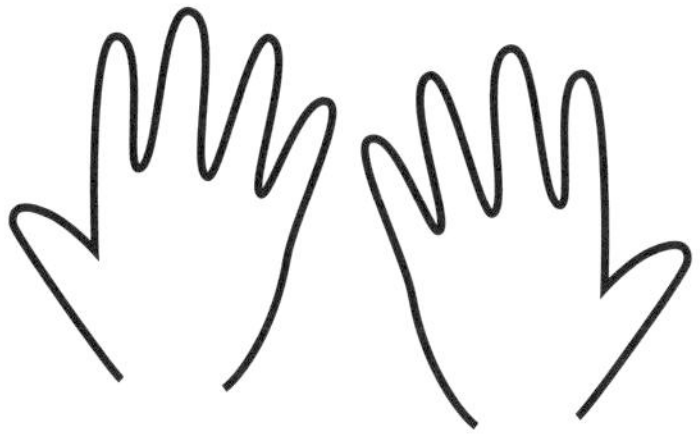

clean

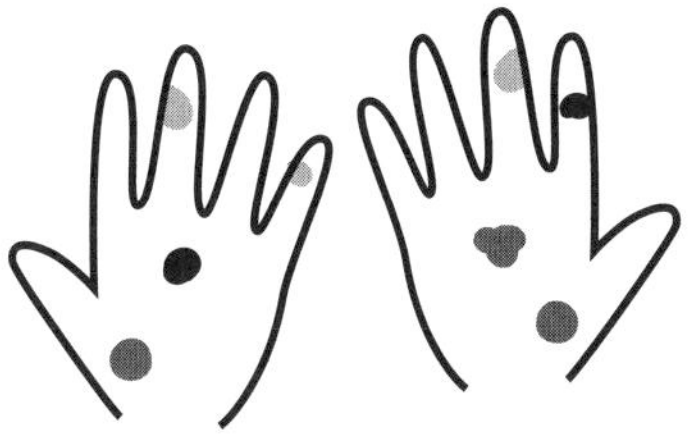

dirty

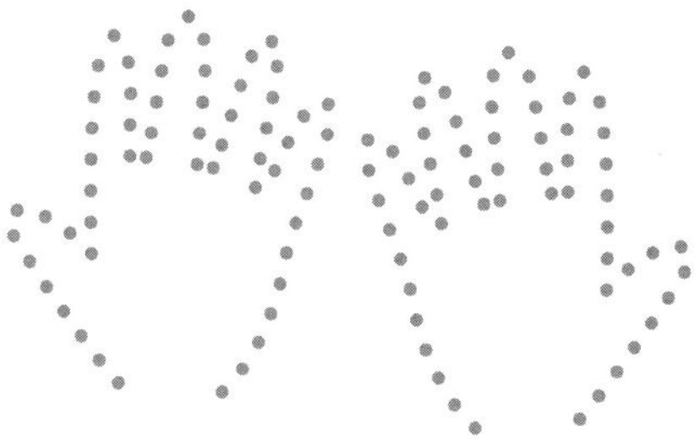

clean

dirty

clean

dirty

clean

dirty

dirty

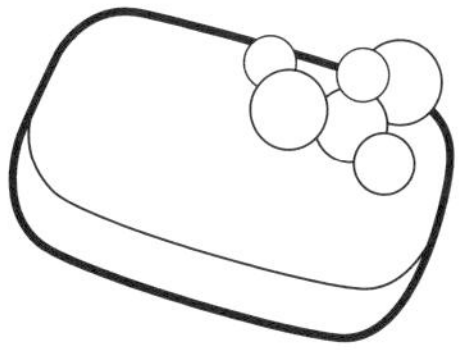

wash

clean

dirty

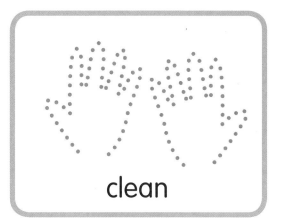

wash

Write 1, 2, 3, and 4.

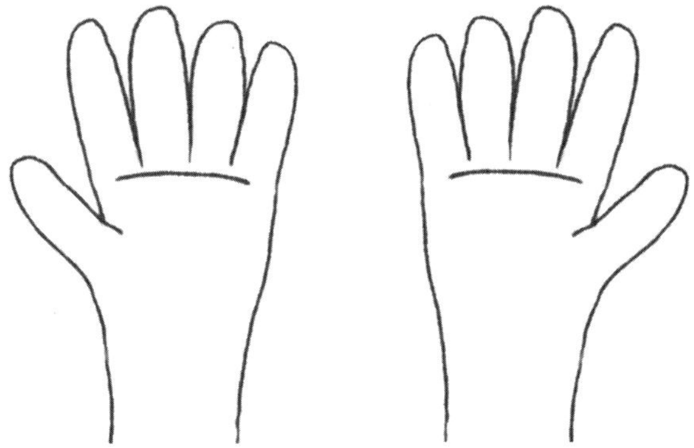

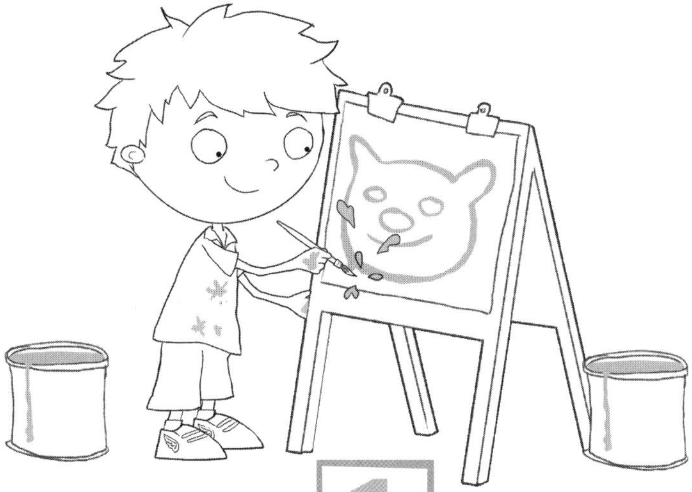

1

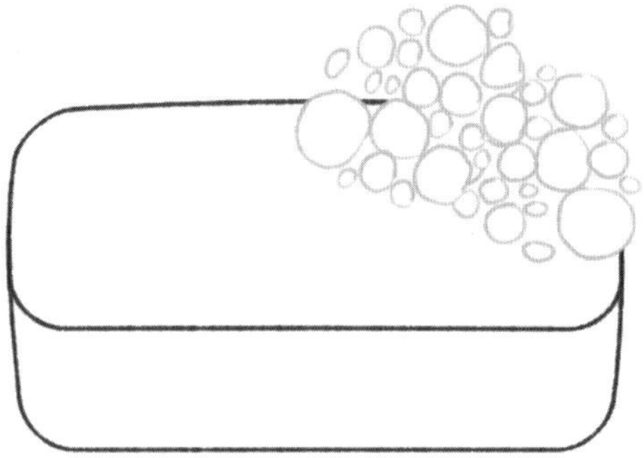

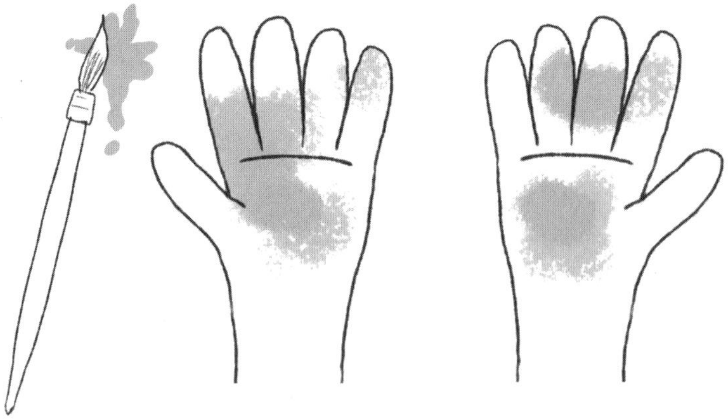

Circle the monster that is different.

Look and circle 6 differences in Picture 2.

1

2

Look, trace, and match.

happy

sad

sad

happy

Count and circle the number.

9 10

9 10

9 10

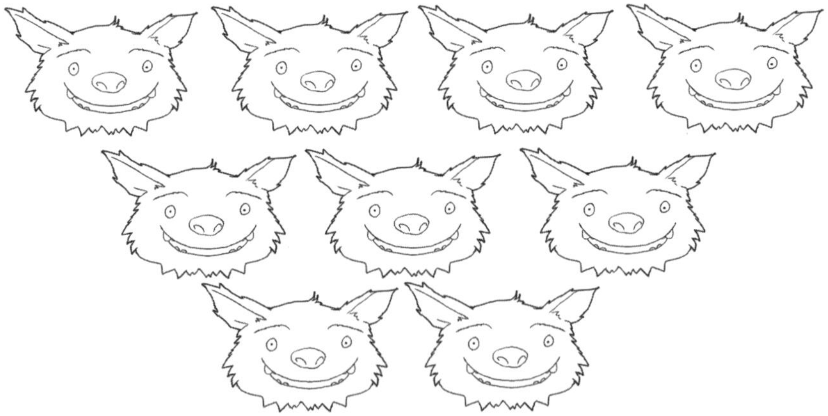

9 10

Trace and color.

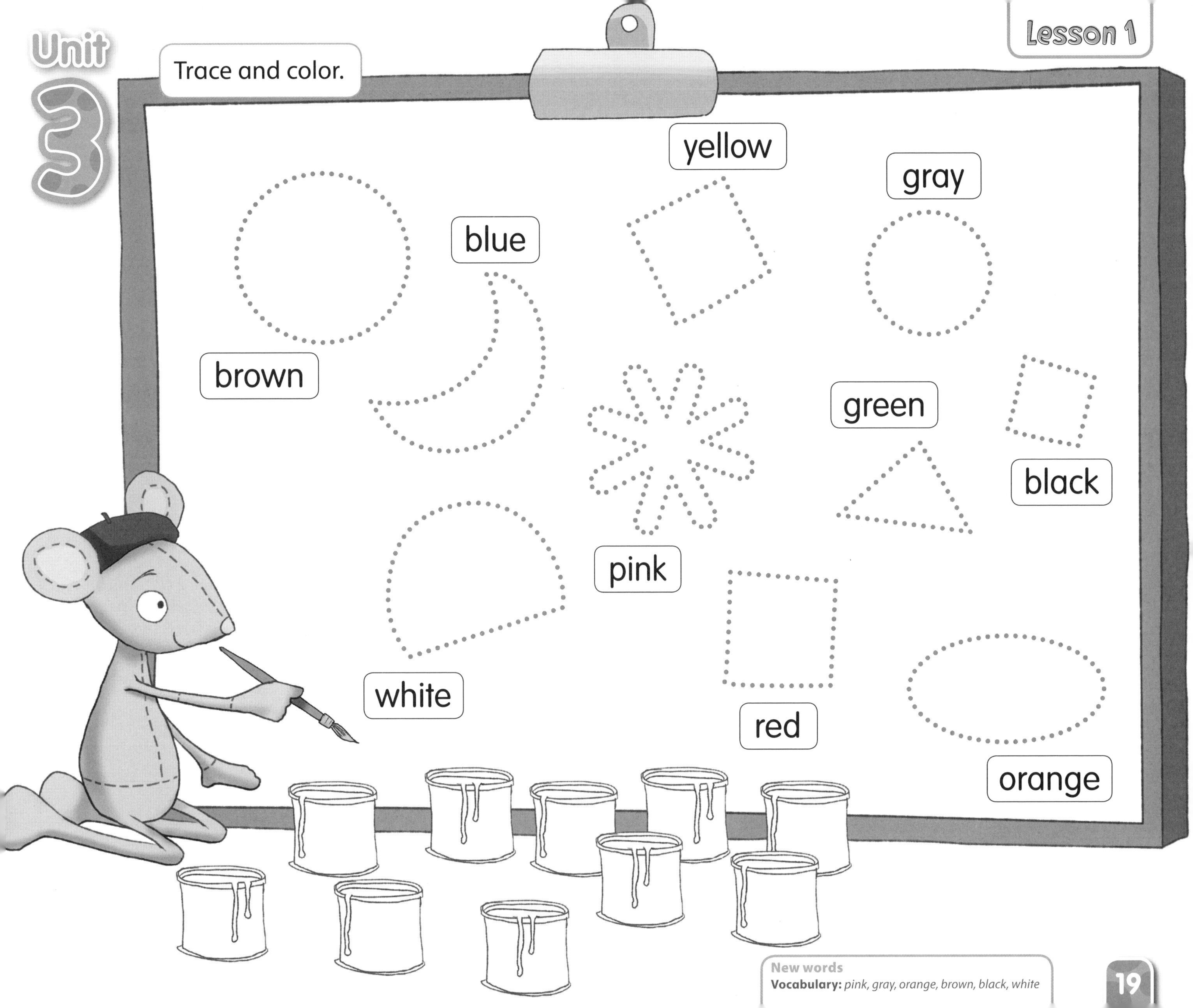
yellow
gray
blue
brown
green
black
pink
white
red
orange

New words
Vocabulary: *pink, gray, orange, brown, black, white*

Look and circle 6 differences in Picture 2.

1

2

Story **Structure:** *What color is it? It's …*
Vocabulary: colors

Read and color. Say *It's gray.*

gray

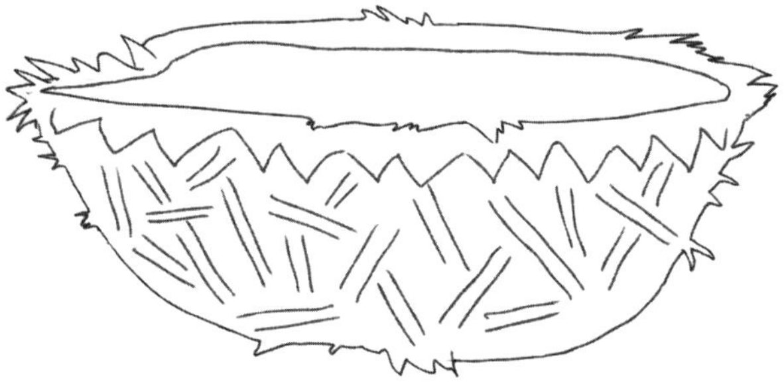

brown

orange

pink

white

black

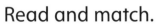

Read and match.

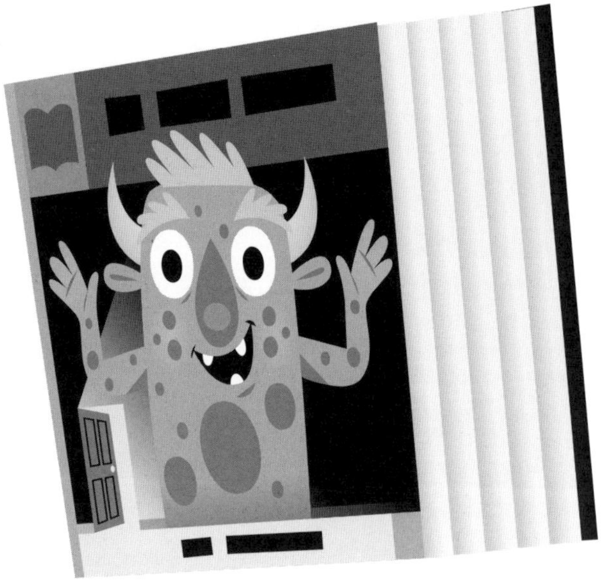

big

small

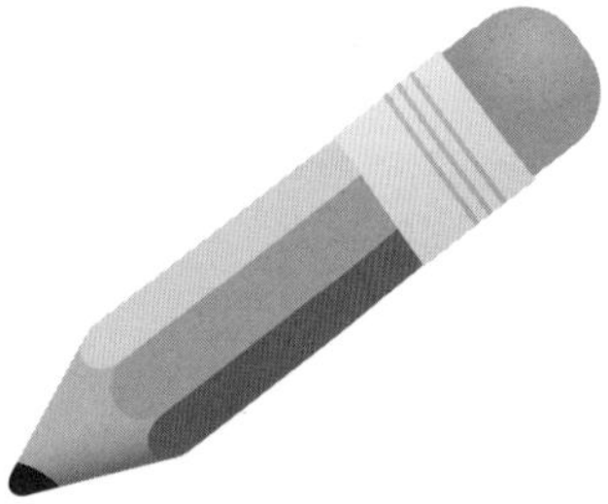

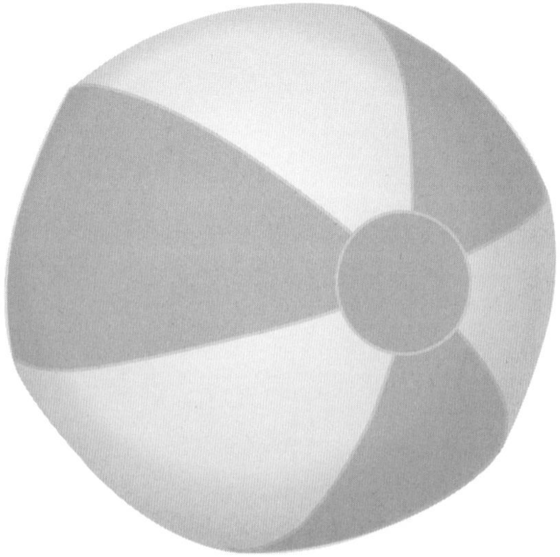

Smart topic **Big and small**
Vocabulary: *book, big, pencil, small*

Look and draw.

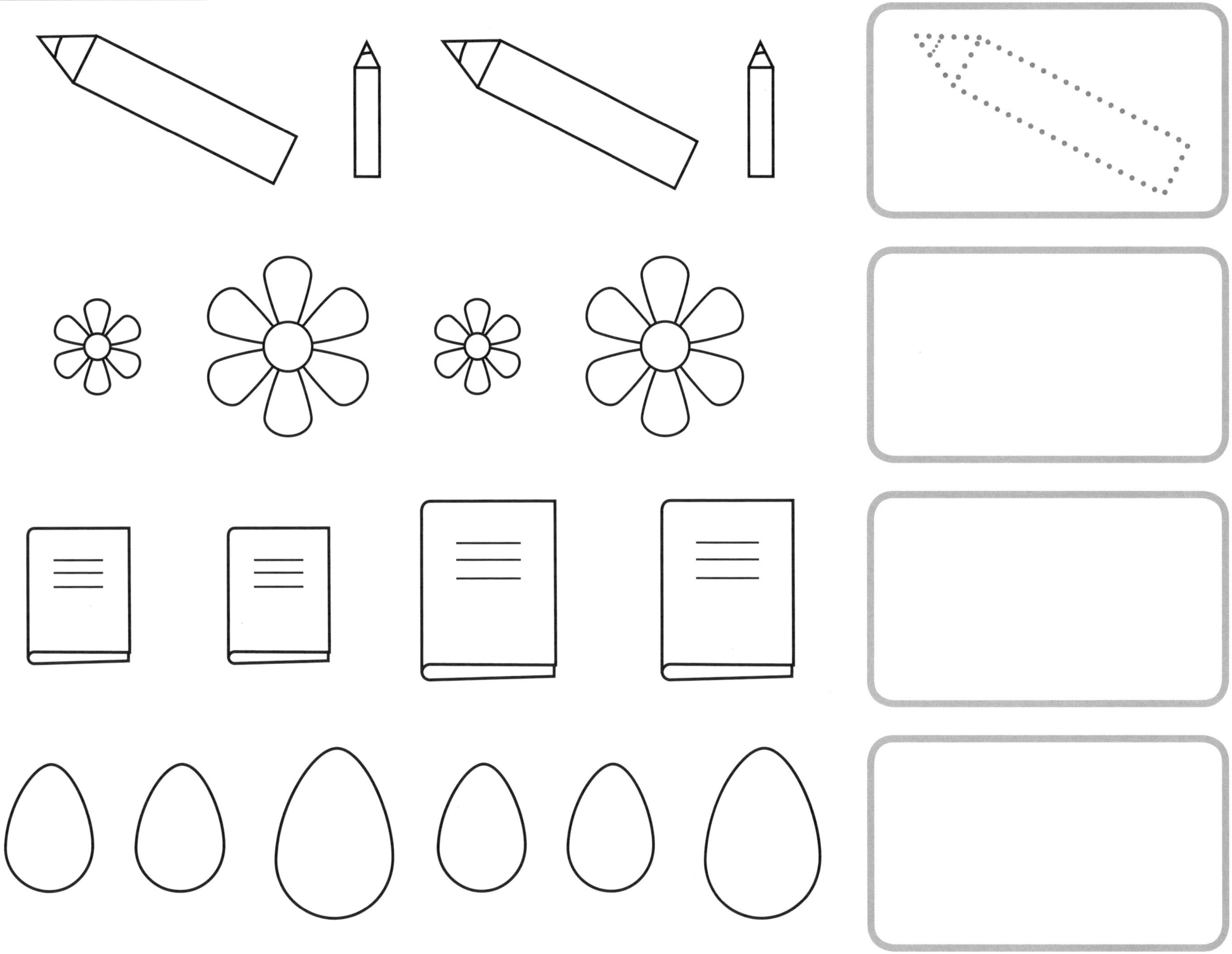

Trace and color. Draw a picture.

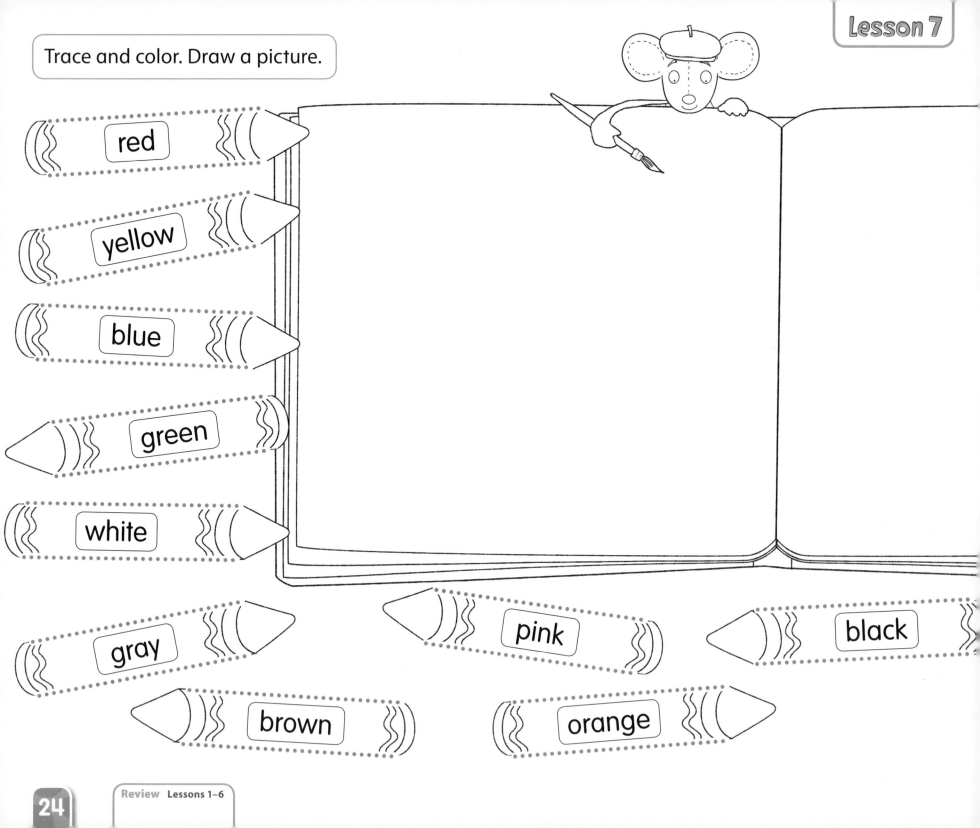

red

yellow

blue

green

white

gray

pink

black

brown

orange

Count, write, and color.

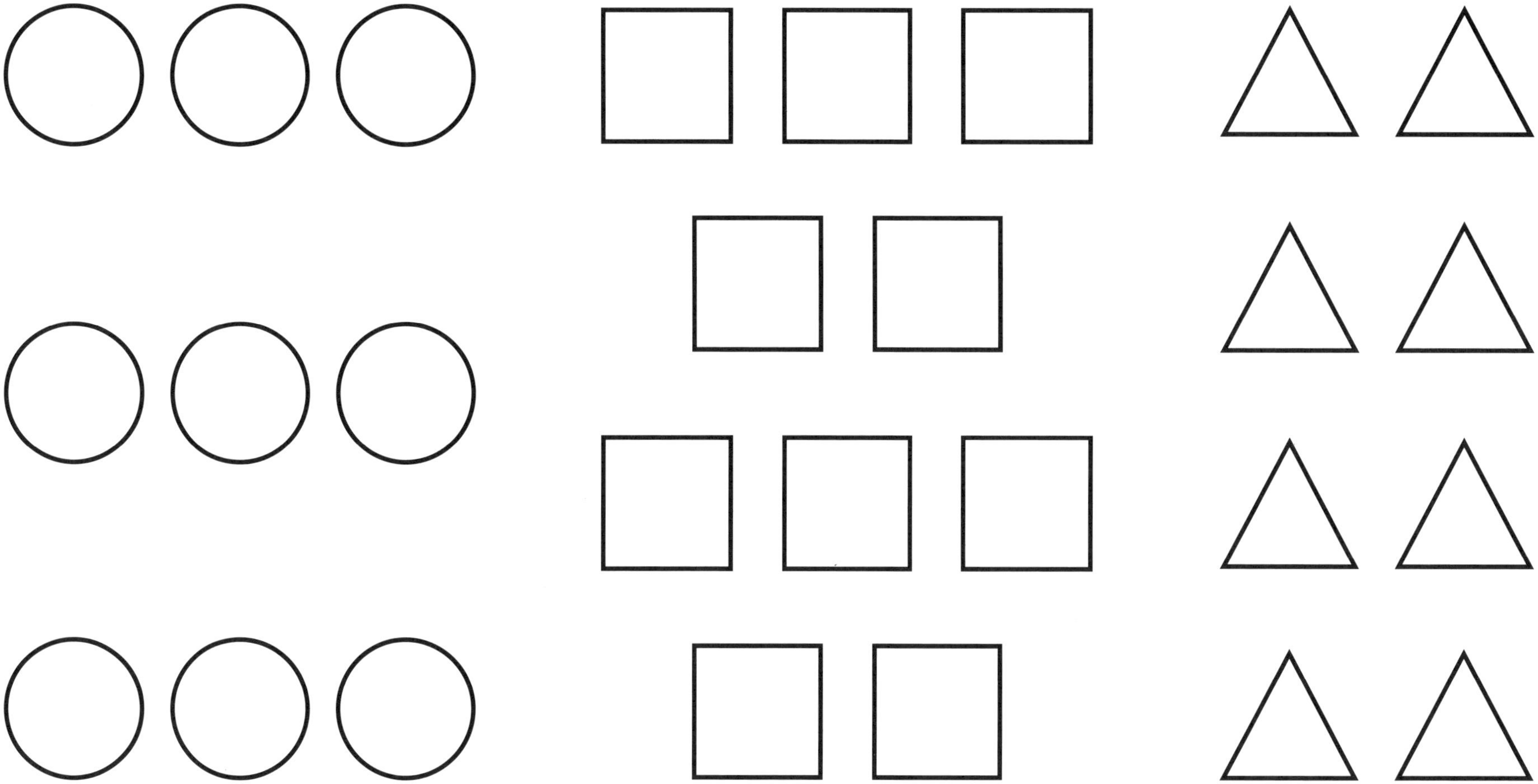

● 9 circles

■ squares

▲ triangles

Read, trace, and color.

1. pink

2. brown

3. orange

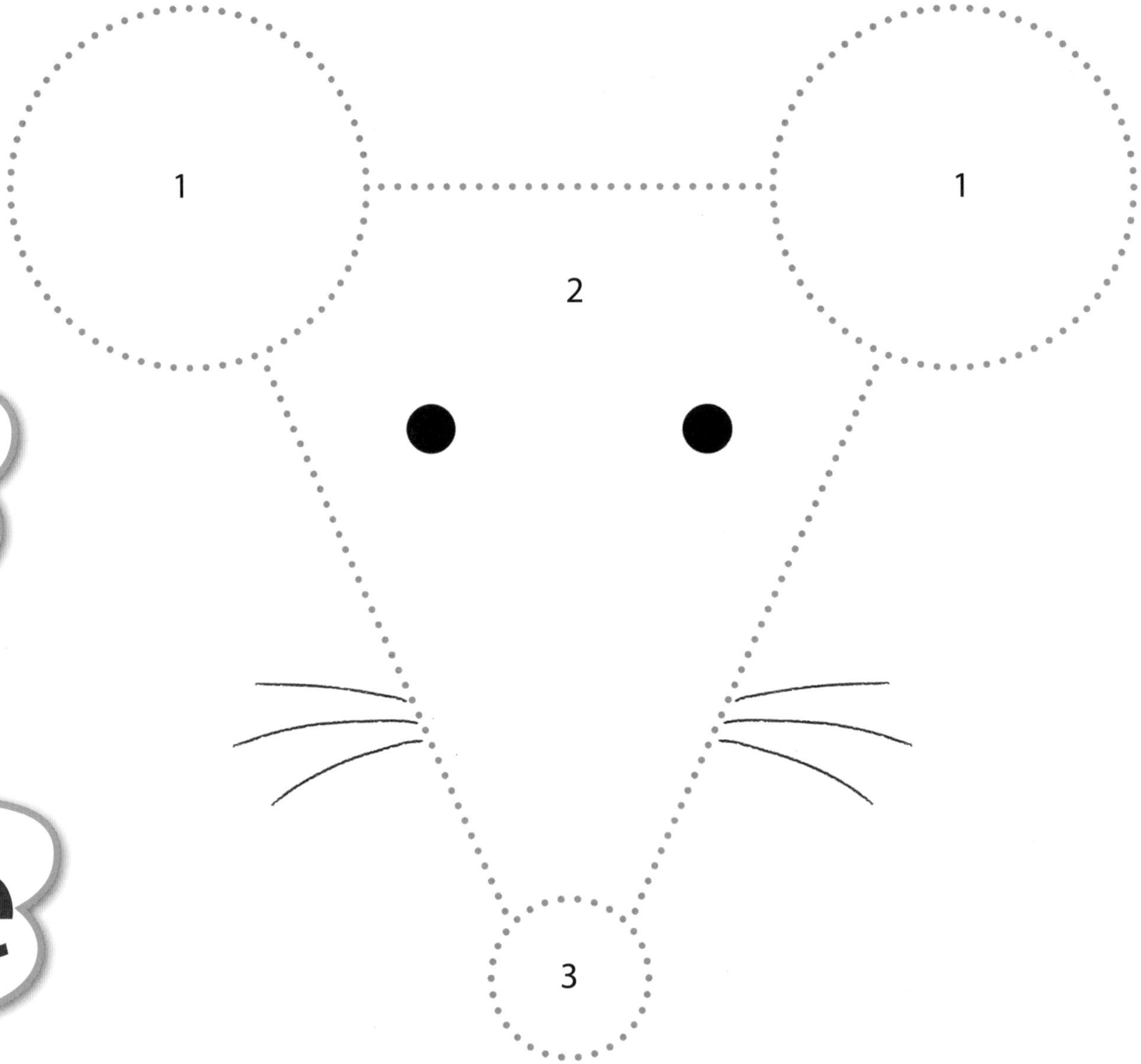
1
1
2
3

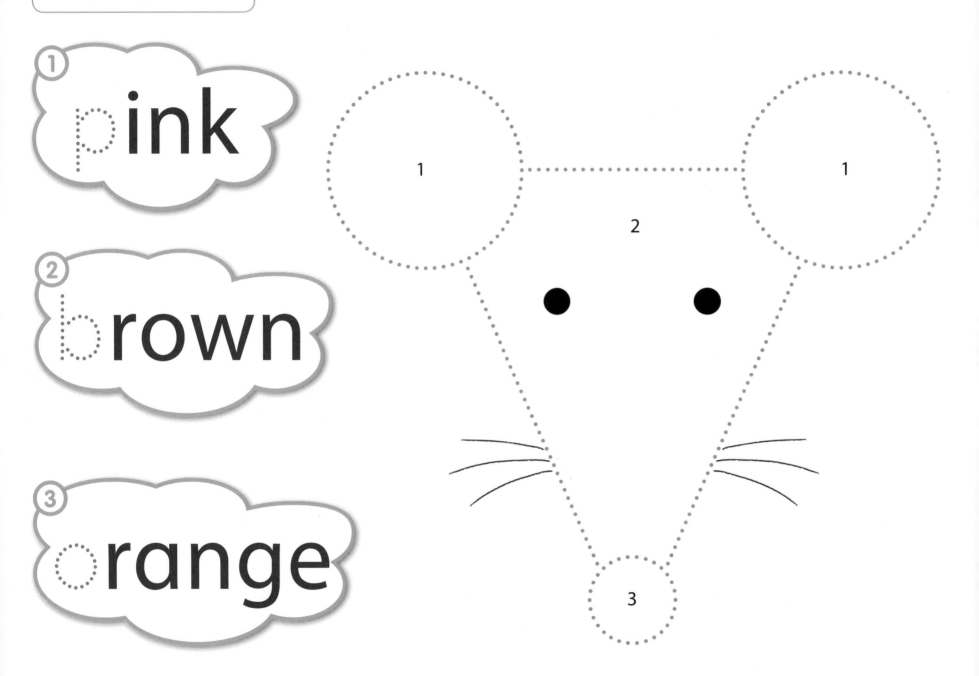

Literacy Tracing initial letters
Vocabulary: colors

Count, write, and circle.

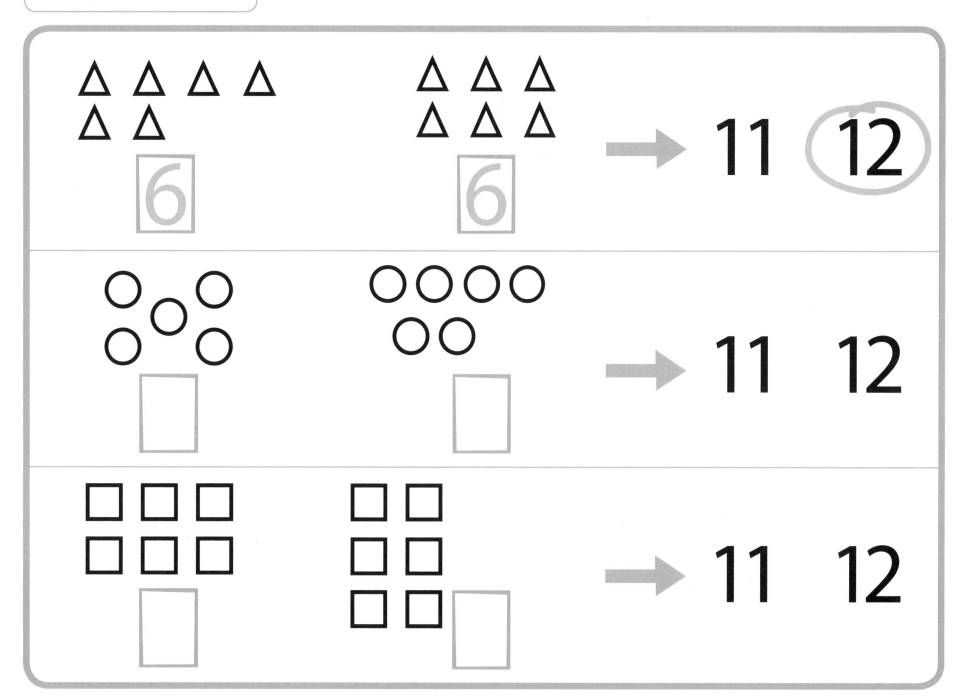

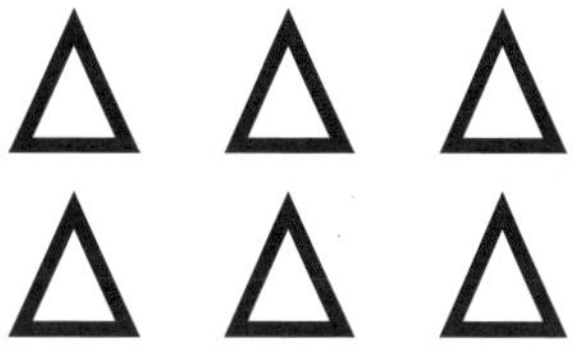

6 6 → 11 (12)

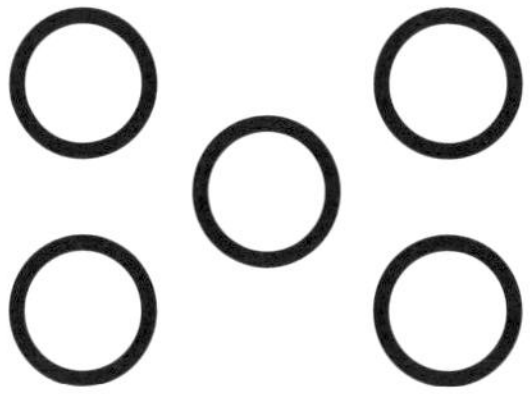
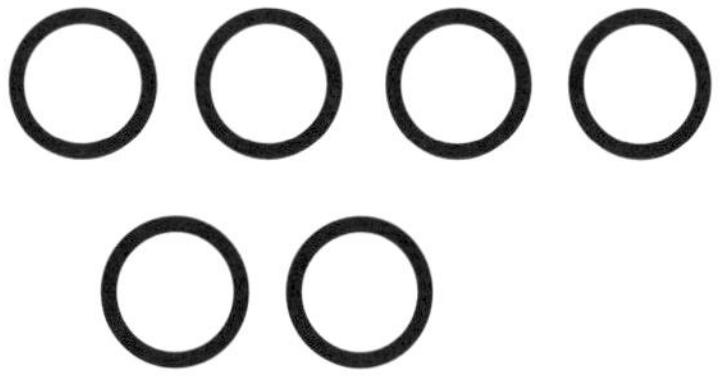

→ 11 12

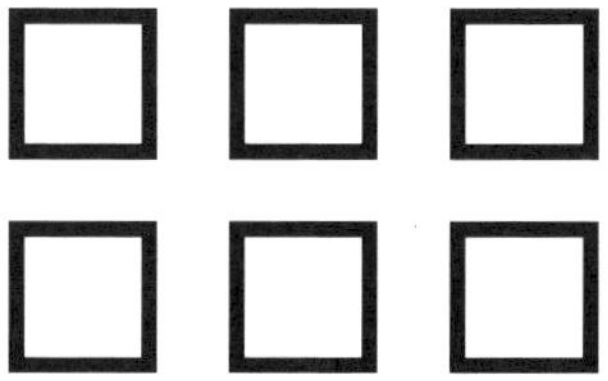
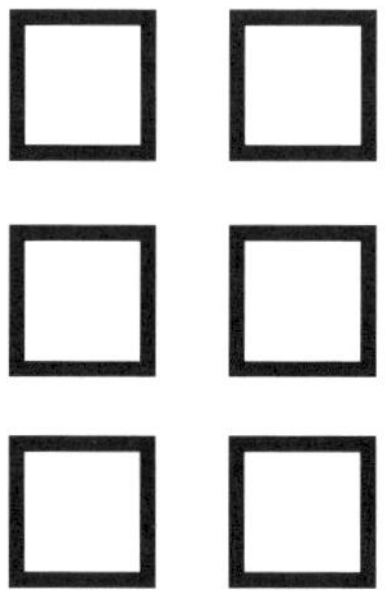

→ 11 12

Match and color.

father

mother

sister

grandfather

grandmother

brother

New words

Vocabulary: *mother, father, sister, brother, grandmother, grandfather*

Trace and color. Say *Pull, pull, pull!*

Read and trace. Say *Here's my mother.*

1

mother

2

father

3

sister

4

brother

5

grandmother

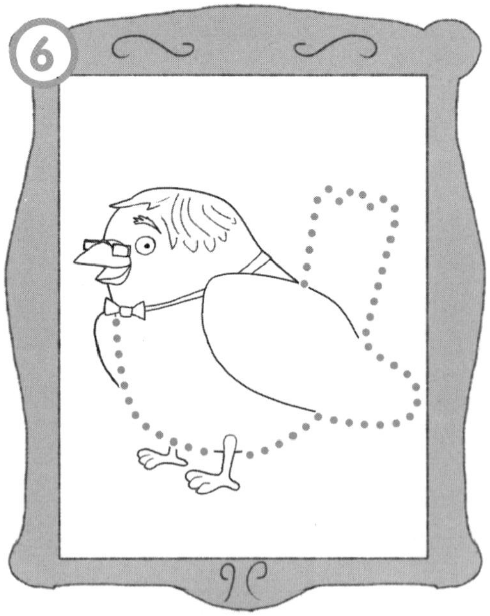
6

grandfather

Story **Structure:** *Here's my …*
Vocabulary: family

Trace, color, and say.

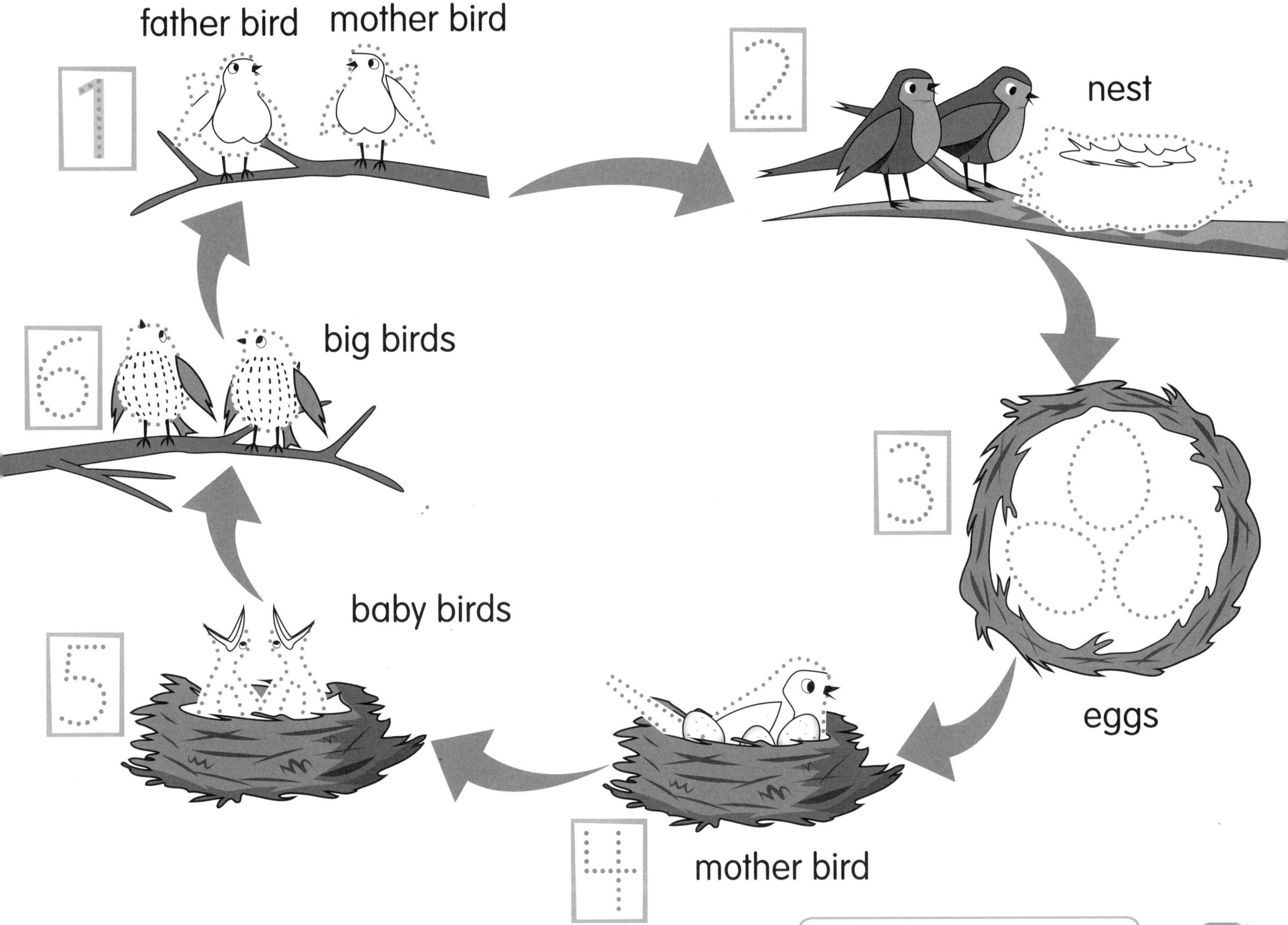
father bird
mother bird
1
2
nest
3
eggs
4
mother bird
5
baby birds
6
big birds

Smart topic Bird life cycle
Vocabulary: *bird, nest, eggs, baby birds*

Count and circle.

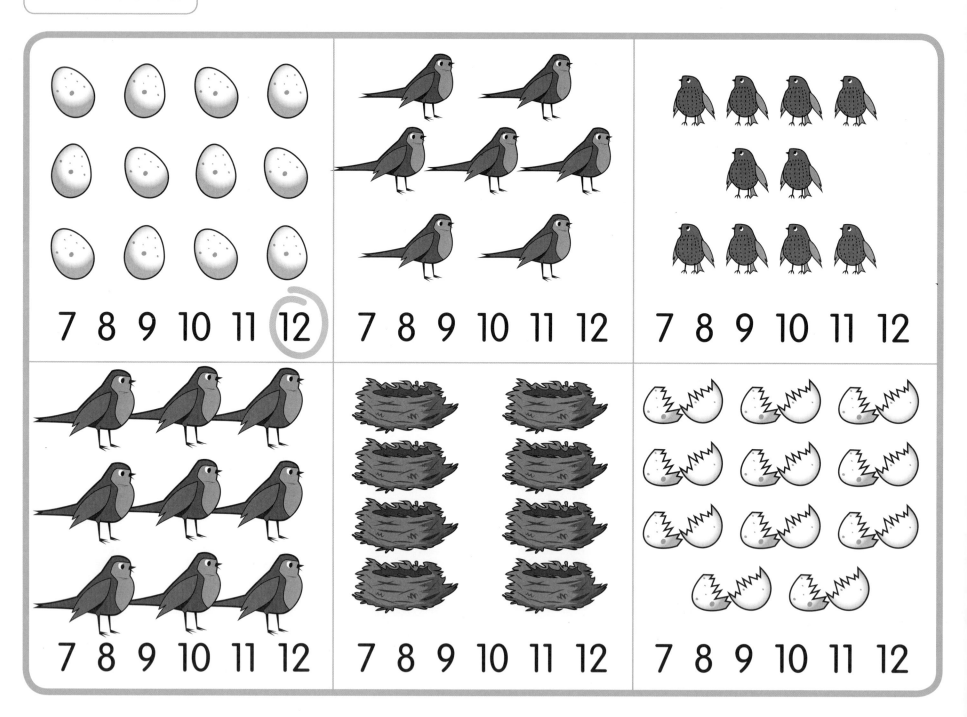

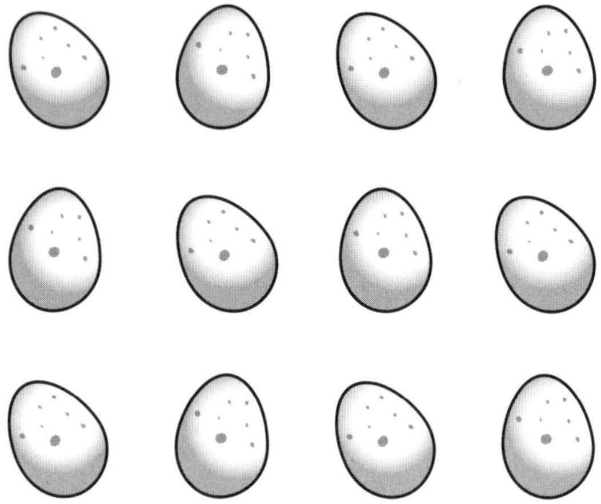

7 8 9 10 11 12

7 8 9 10 11 12

7 8 9 10 11 12

7 8 9 10 11 12

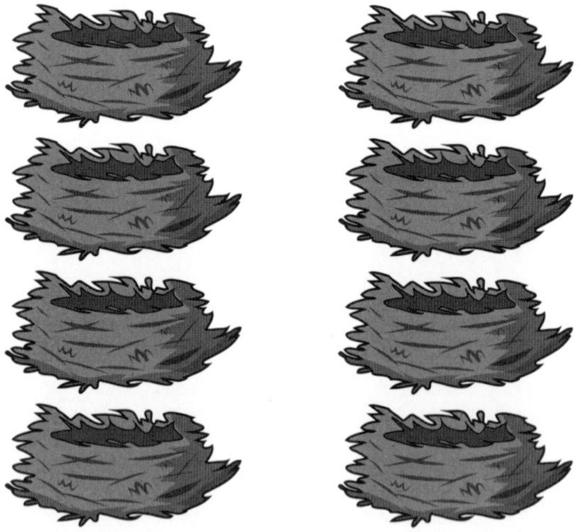

7 8 9 10 11 12

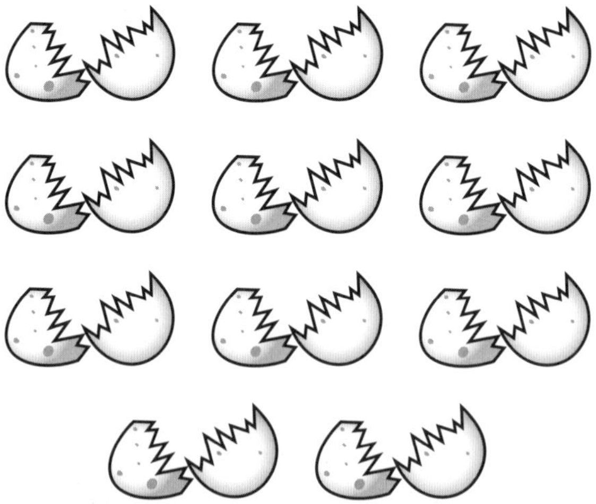

7 8 9 10 11 12

Match and color.

grandfather
mother
father
grandmother
sister
brother

Trace, draw, and color.

My friend and me.

My teacher and me.

My family and me.

Me!

Read, trace, and match.

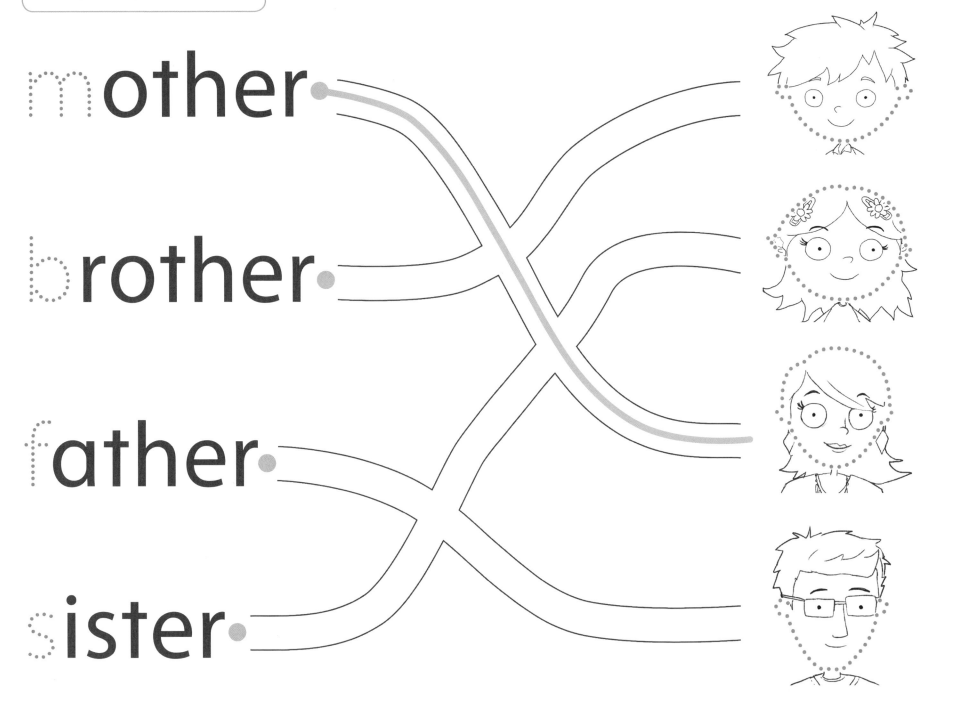

mother

brother

father

sister

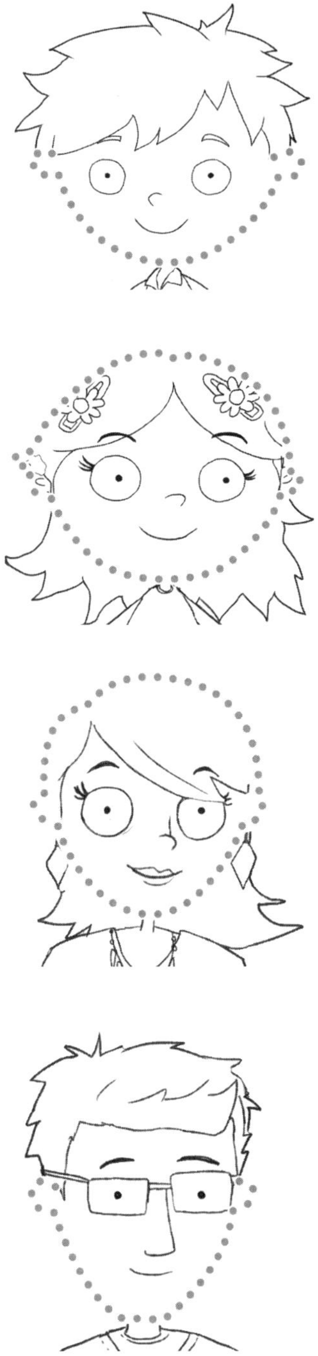

Follow the numbers.

3
4
2
5
10
9
1
6
6
7
12
14
8
12
9
13
11
10

Trace and color.

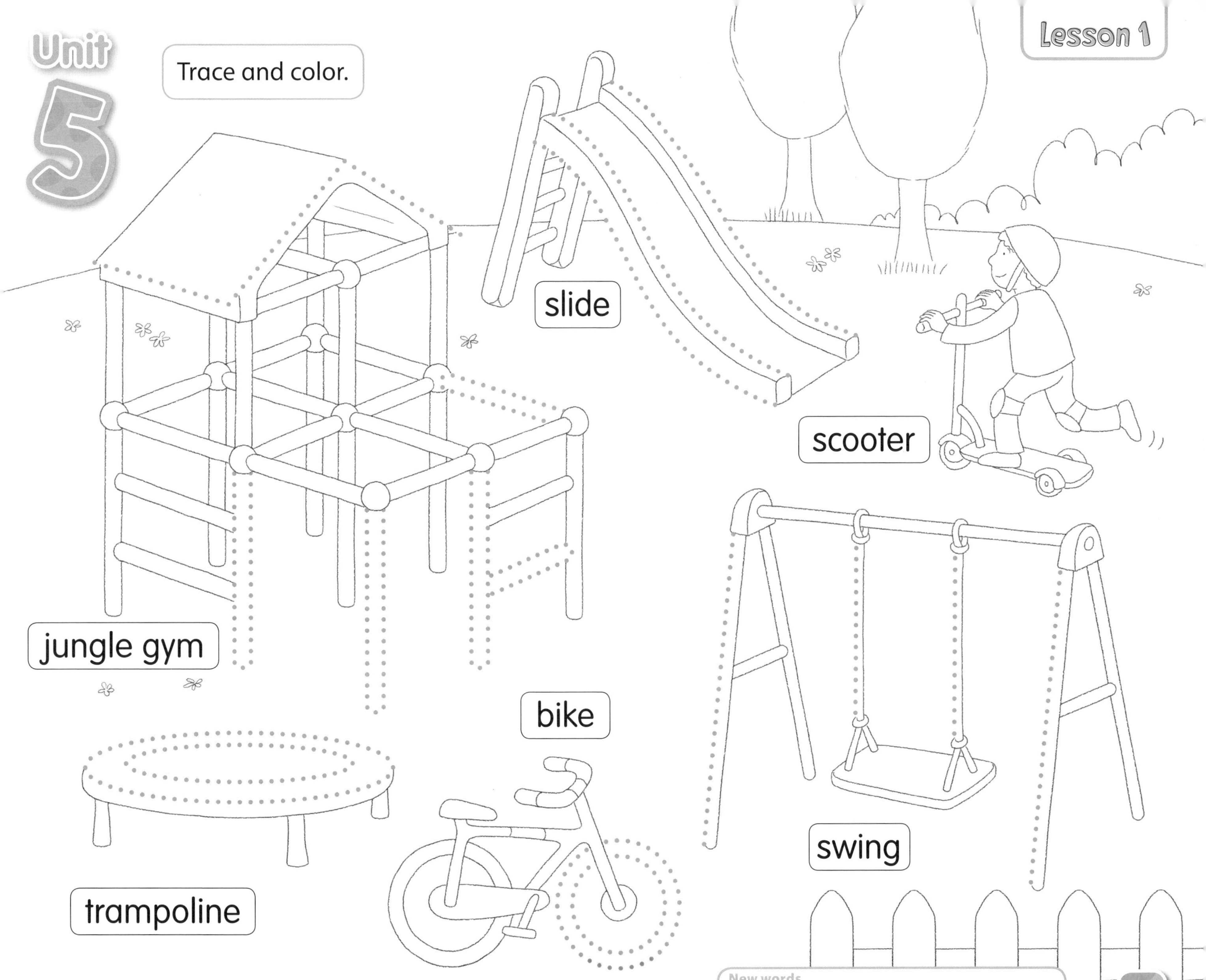
slide
scooter
jungle gym
bike
swing
trampoline

New words

Vocabulary: *slide, swing, jungle gym, bike, scooter, trampoline*

Find and circle 6 differences in Picture 2.

1

2

Story **Structure:** *Is it a …?*
Vocabulary: outdoor toys

Match and read. Say *Is it a bike? Yes./No.*

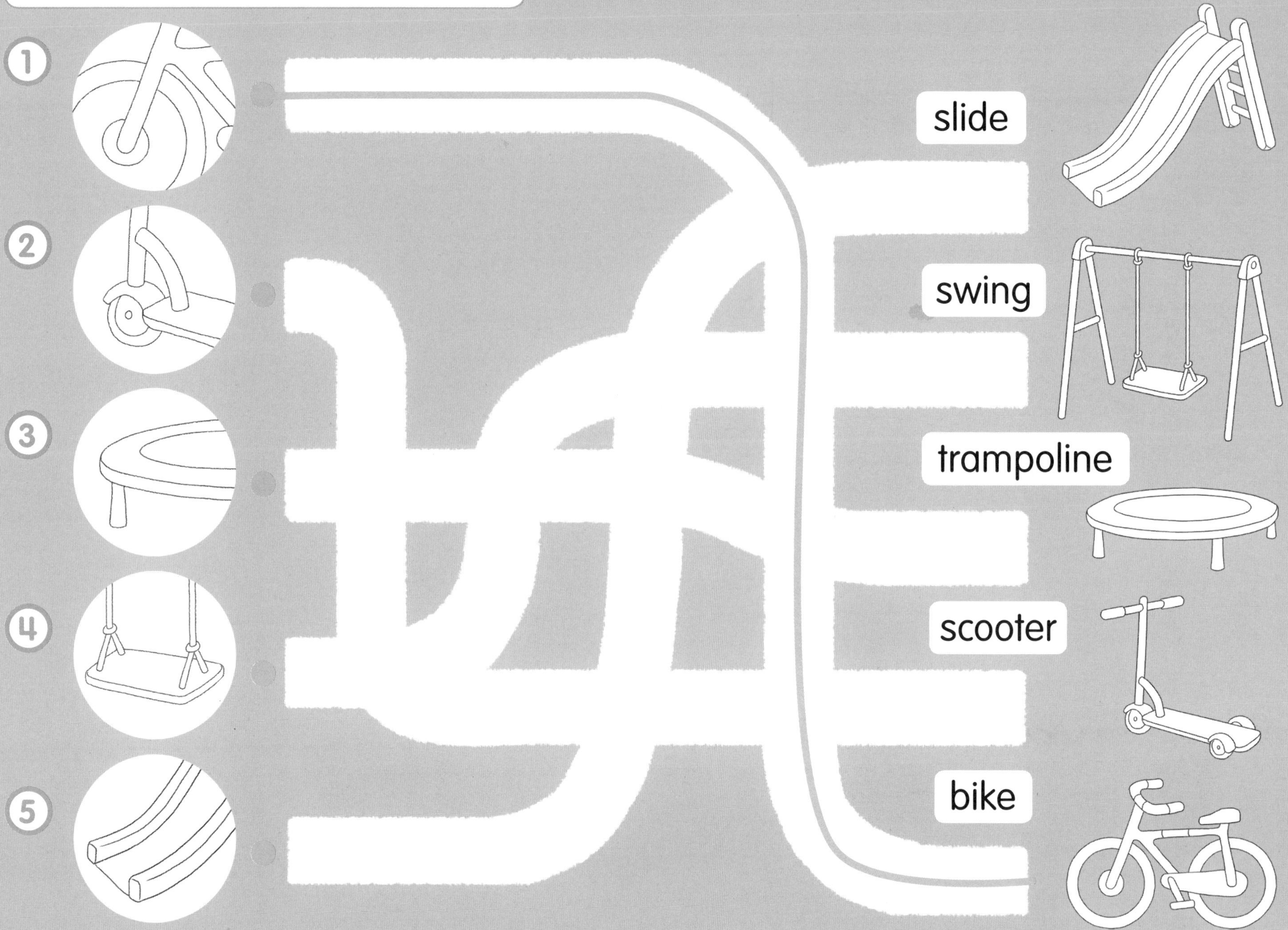
1
2
3
4
5
slide
swing
trampoline
scooter
bike

Look and circle the one that is different.

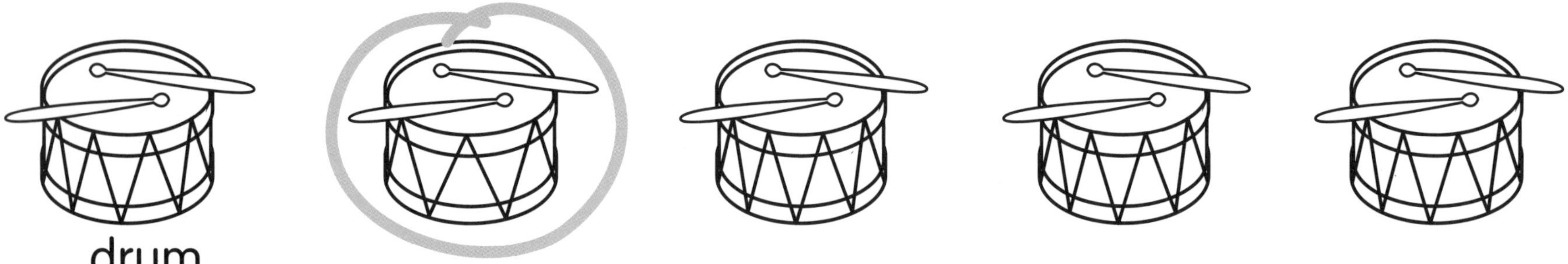

drum

trumpet

guitar

piano

Count and match.

8   10   12   14

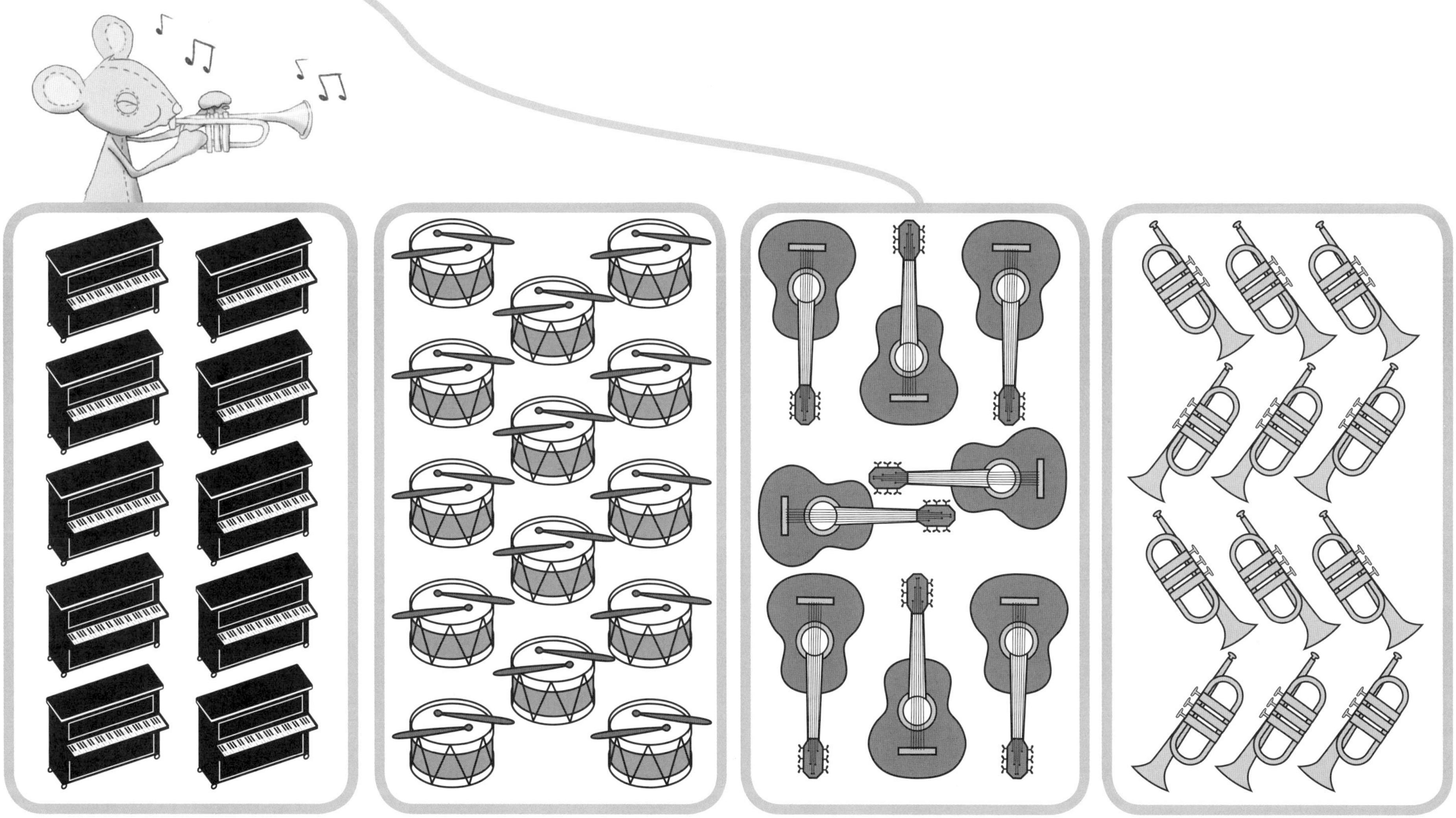

Trace the happy face ( ) if you like the toy or instrument.

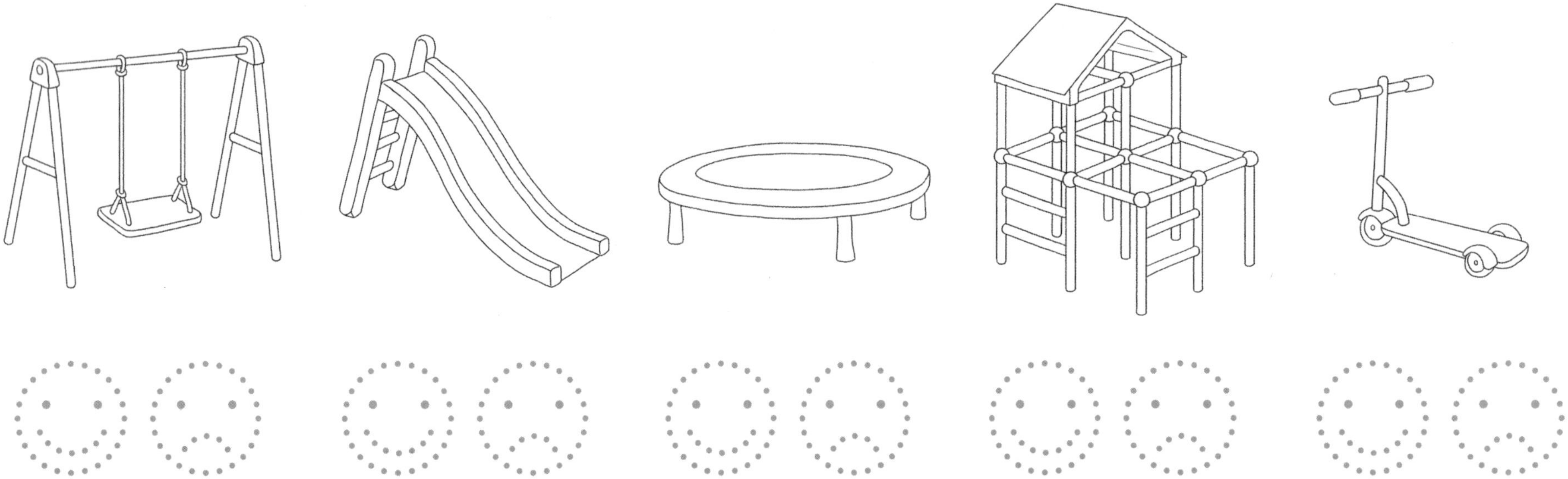

Match and say.

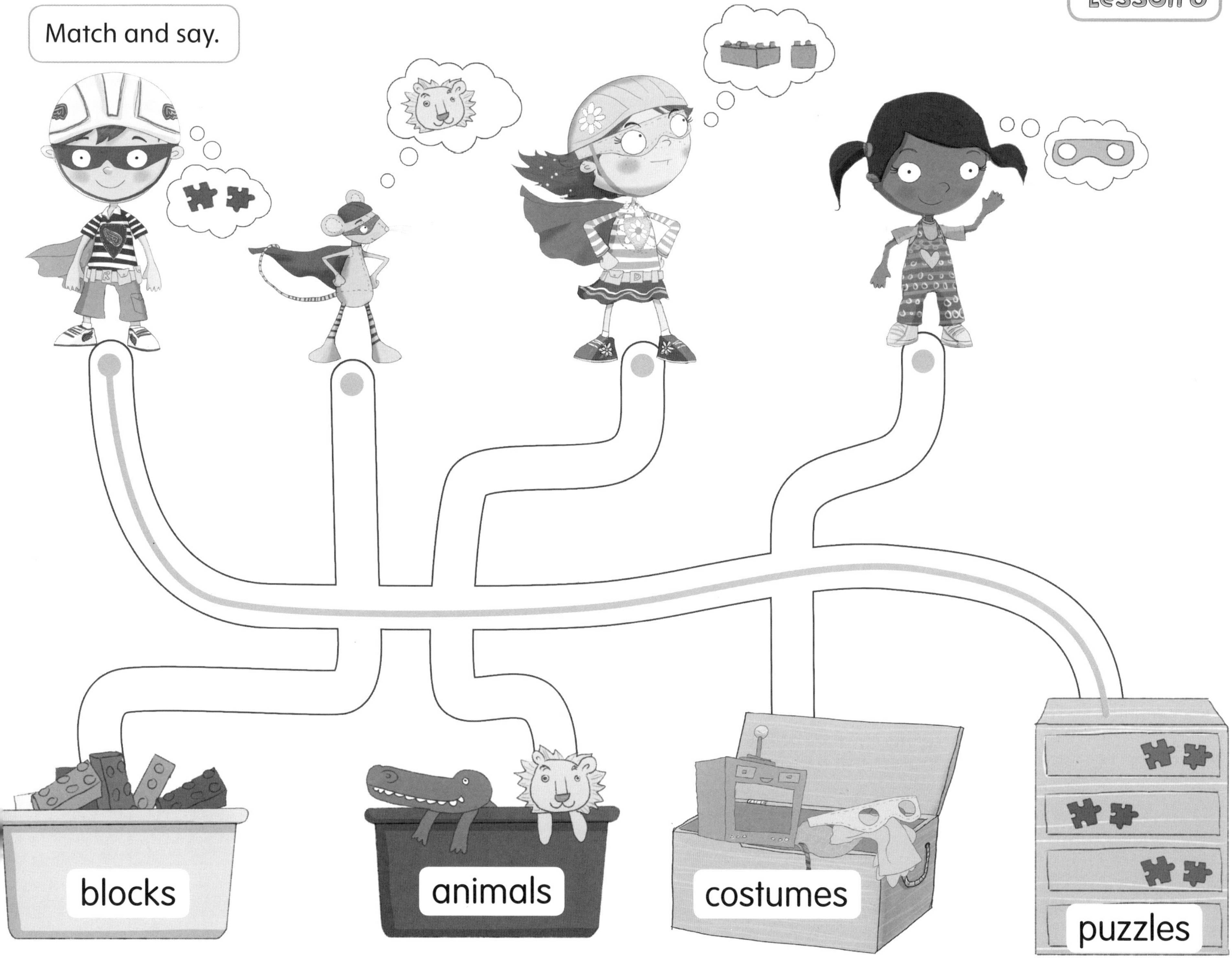
blocks
animals
costumes
puzzles

Read, trace, and circle.

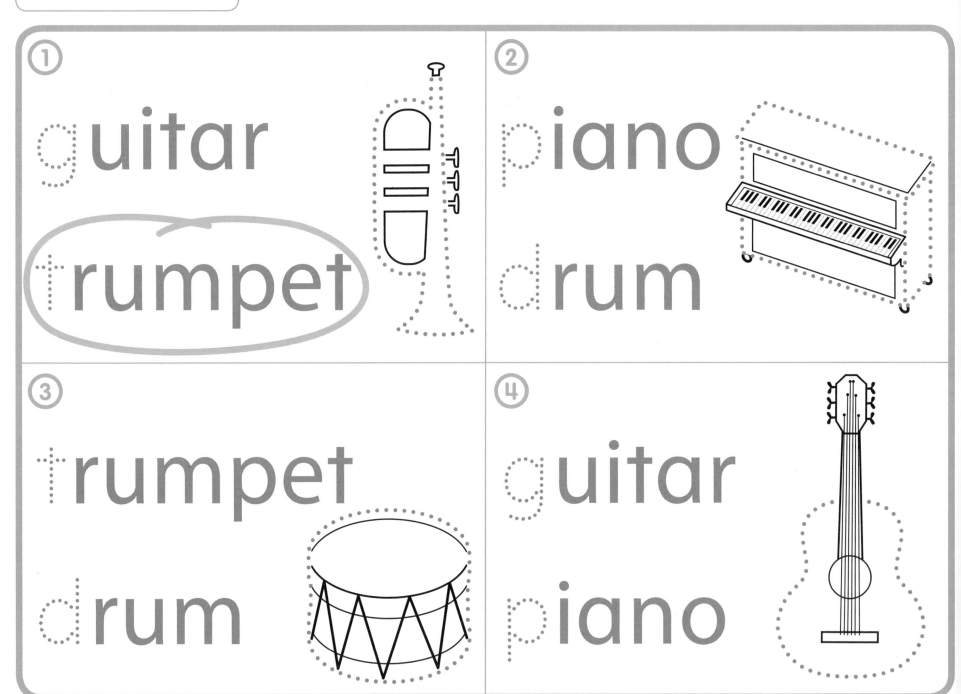

1

guitar

trumpet

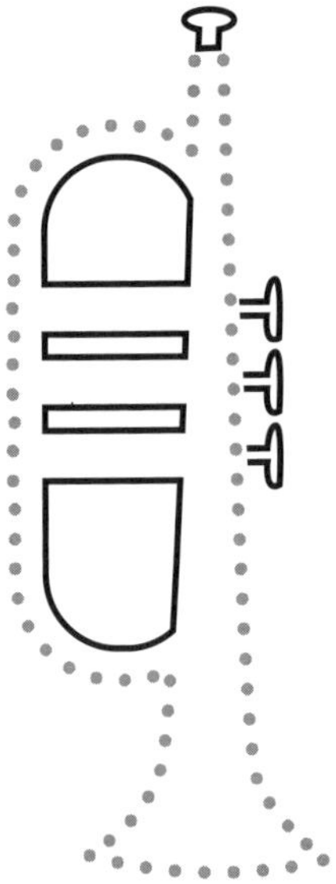

2

piano

drum

3

trumpet

drum

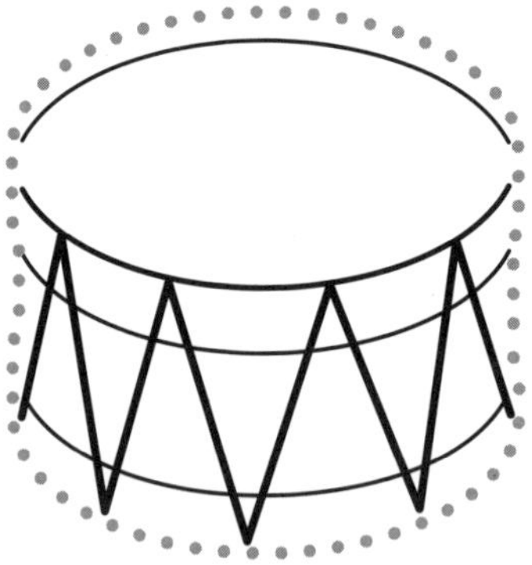

4

guitar

piano

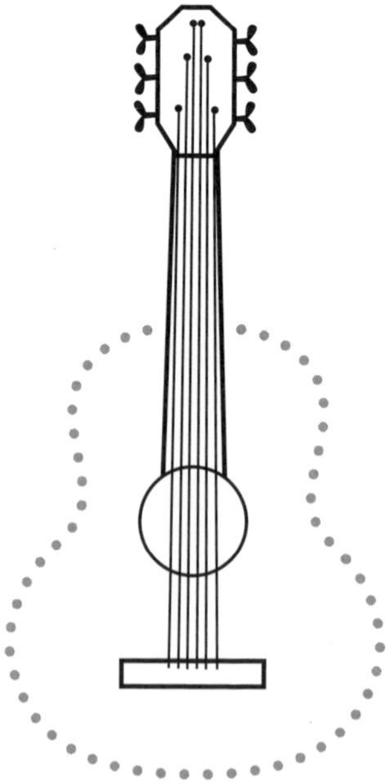

Literacy Word recognition; tracing initial letters
Vocabulary: instruments

Count and trace.

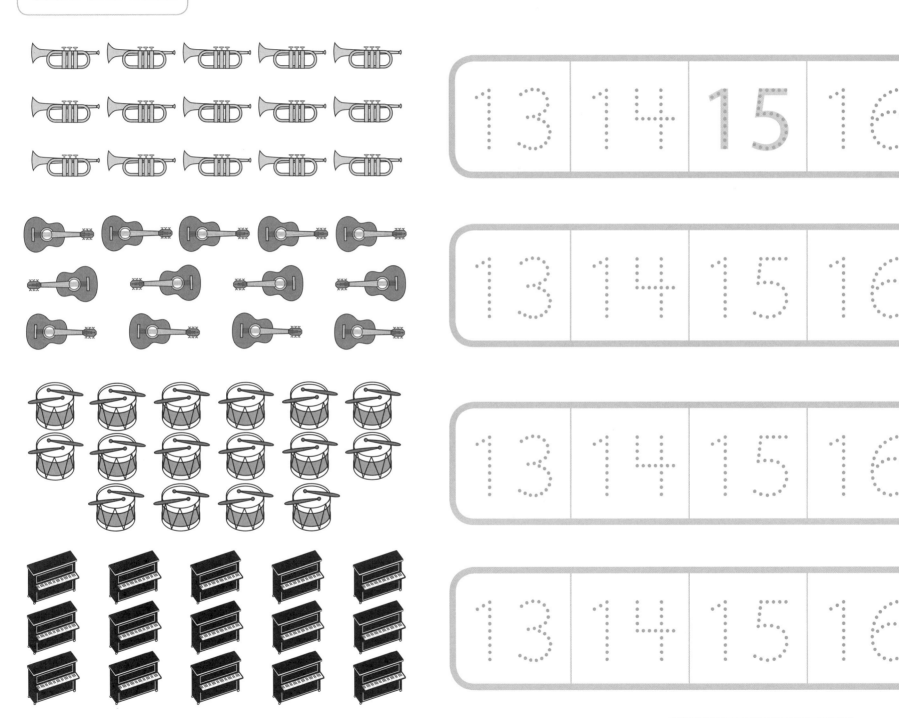

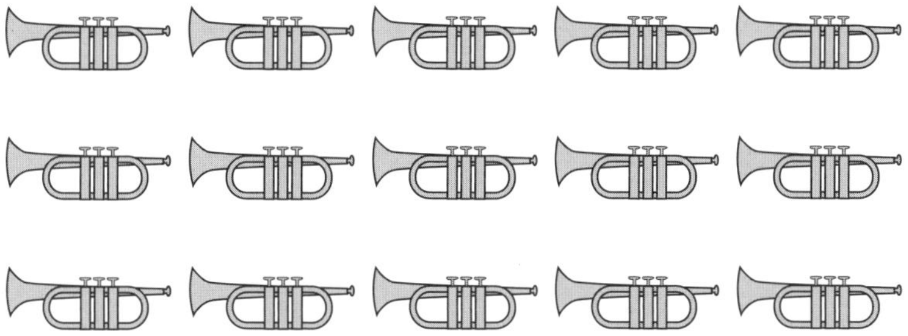

13	14	15	16

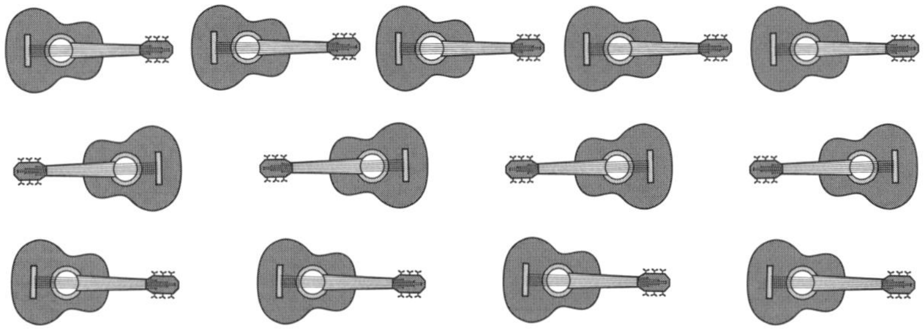

13	14	15	16

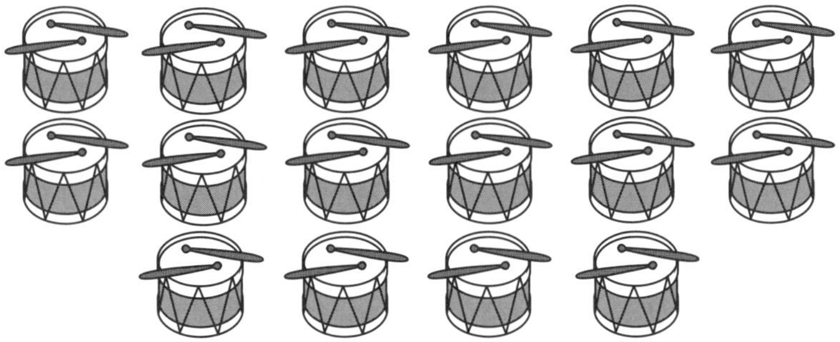

13	14	15	16

13	14	15	16

Match and trace.

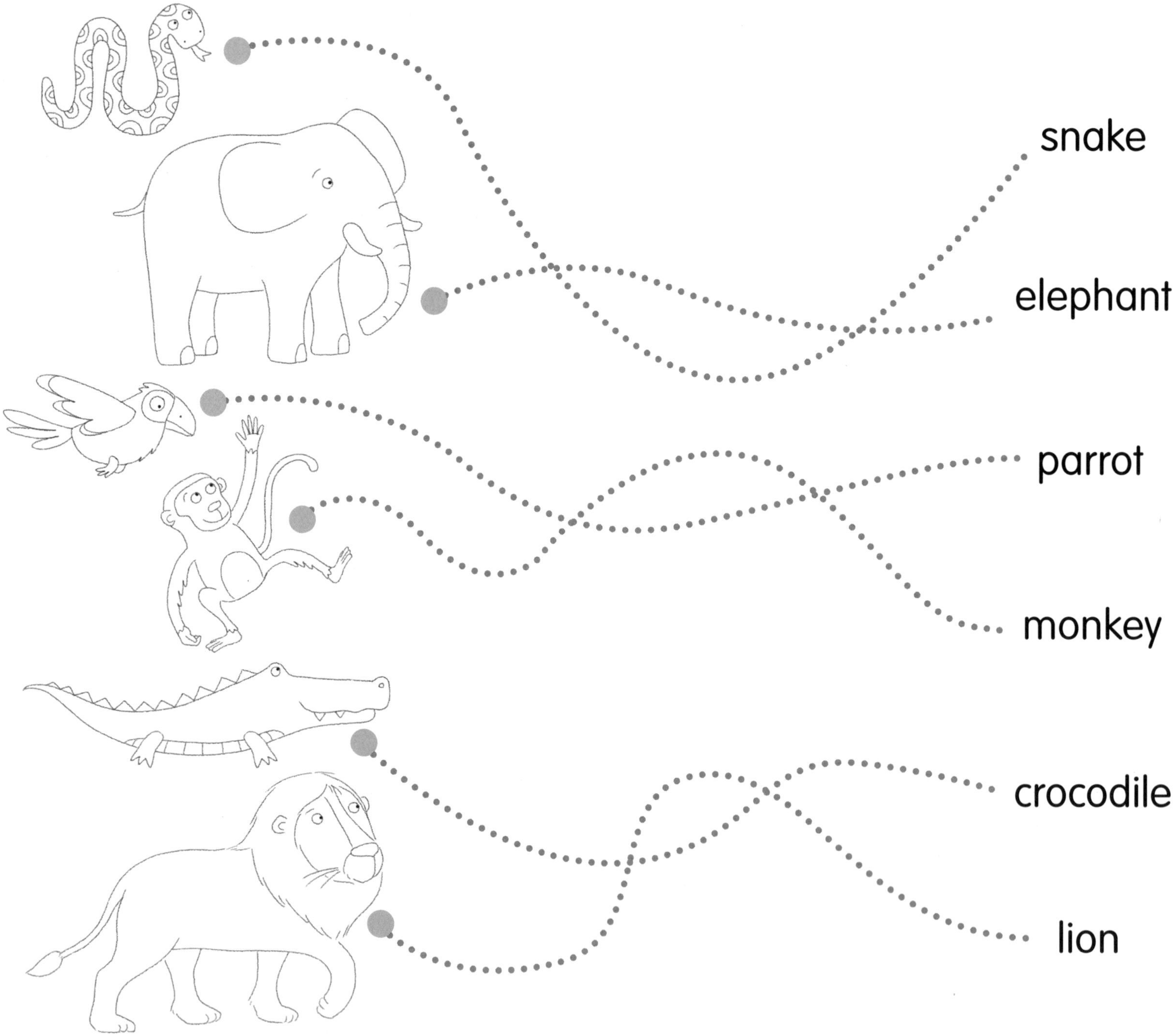
snake
elephant
parrot
monkey
crocodile
lion

New words
Vocabulary: *snake, crocodile, monkey, parrot, lion, elephant*

Look and match.

lion parrot elephant snake monkey crocodile

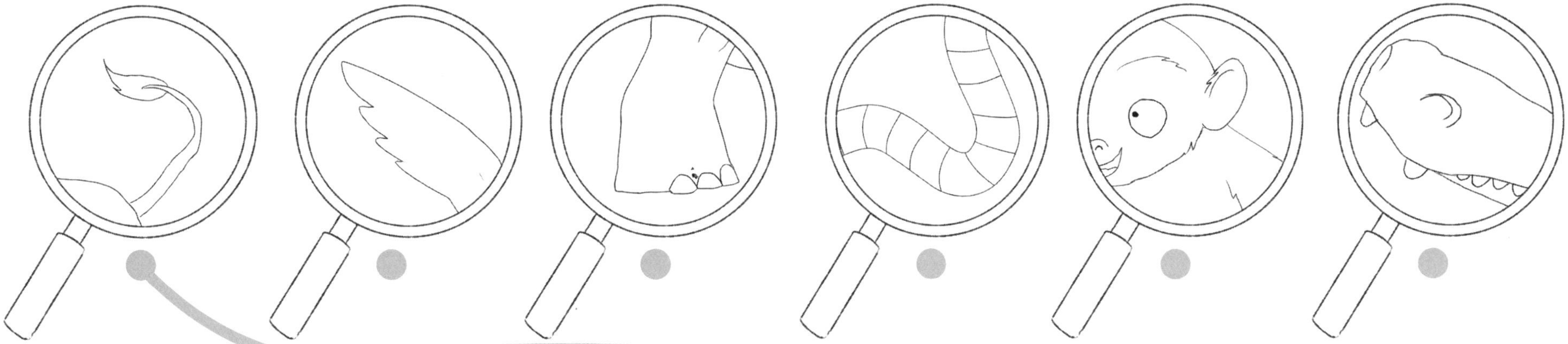

Read and trace. Say *I can see a crocodile.*

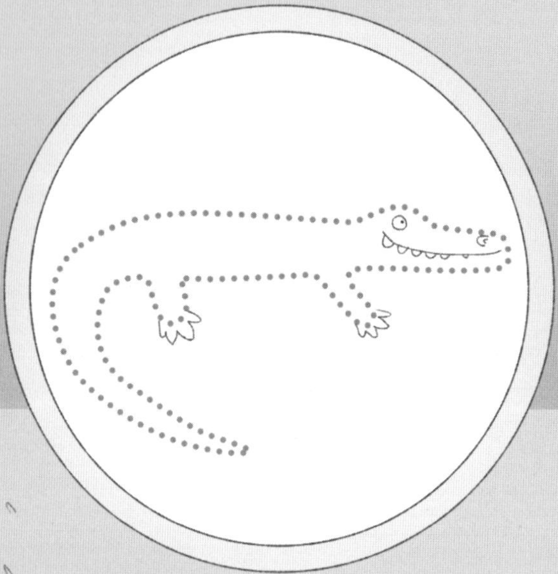

crocodile

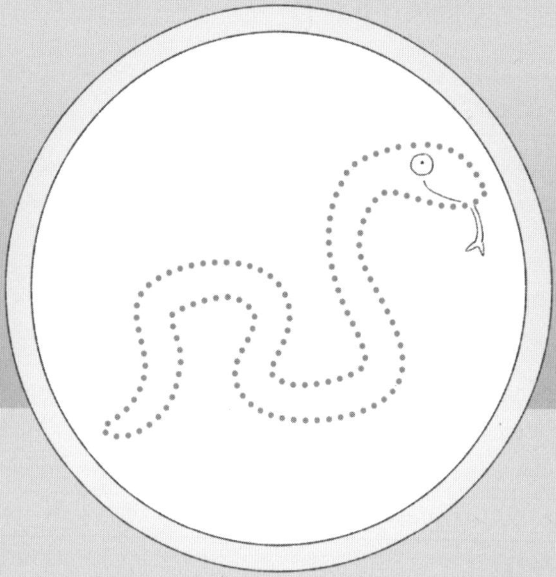

snake

lion

parrot

monkey

Match and trace.

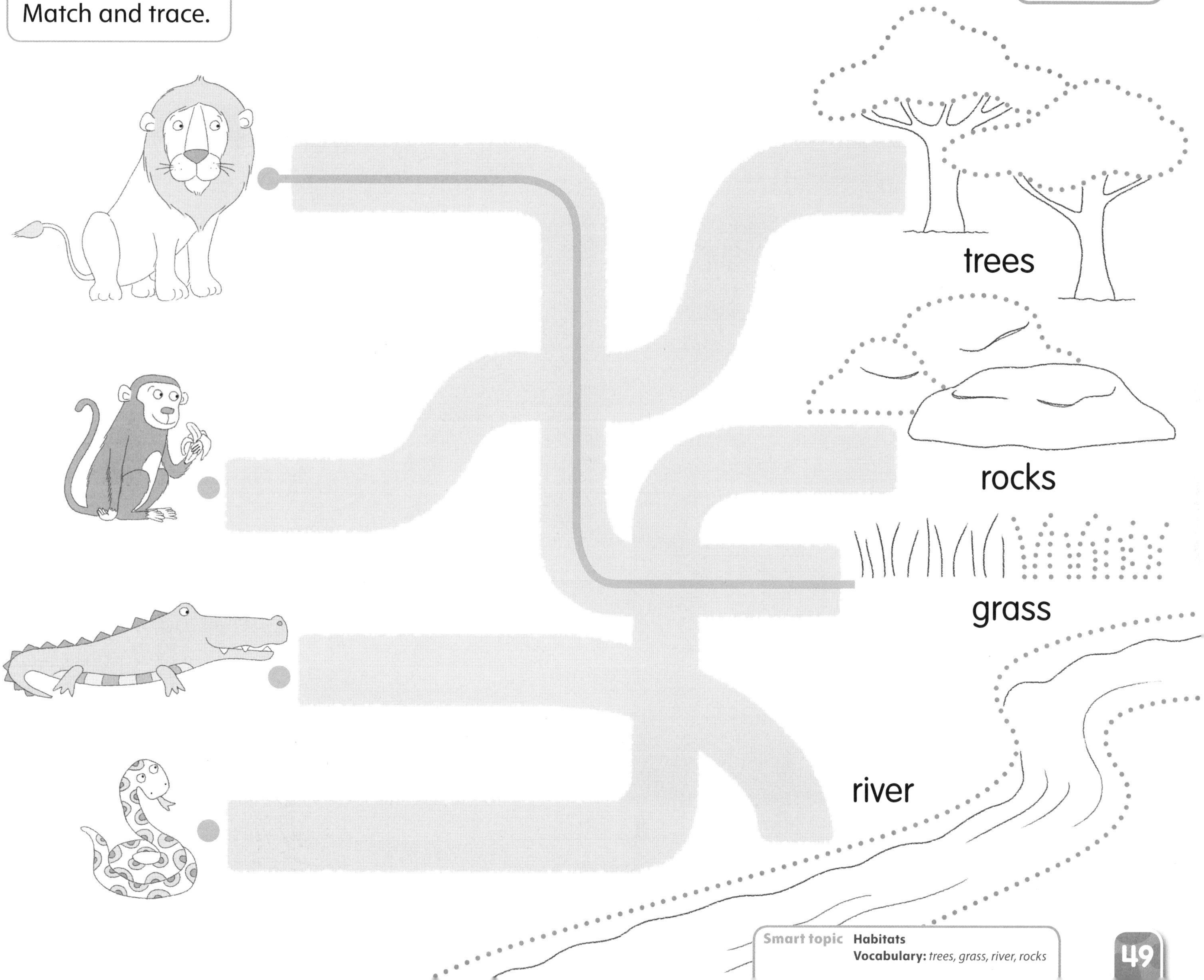
trees
rocks
grass
river

Smart topic **Habitats**
Vocabulary: *trees, grass, river, rocks*

Look and draw.

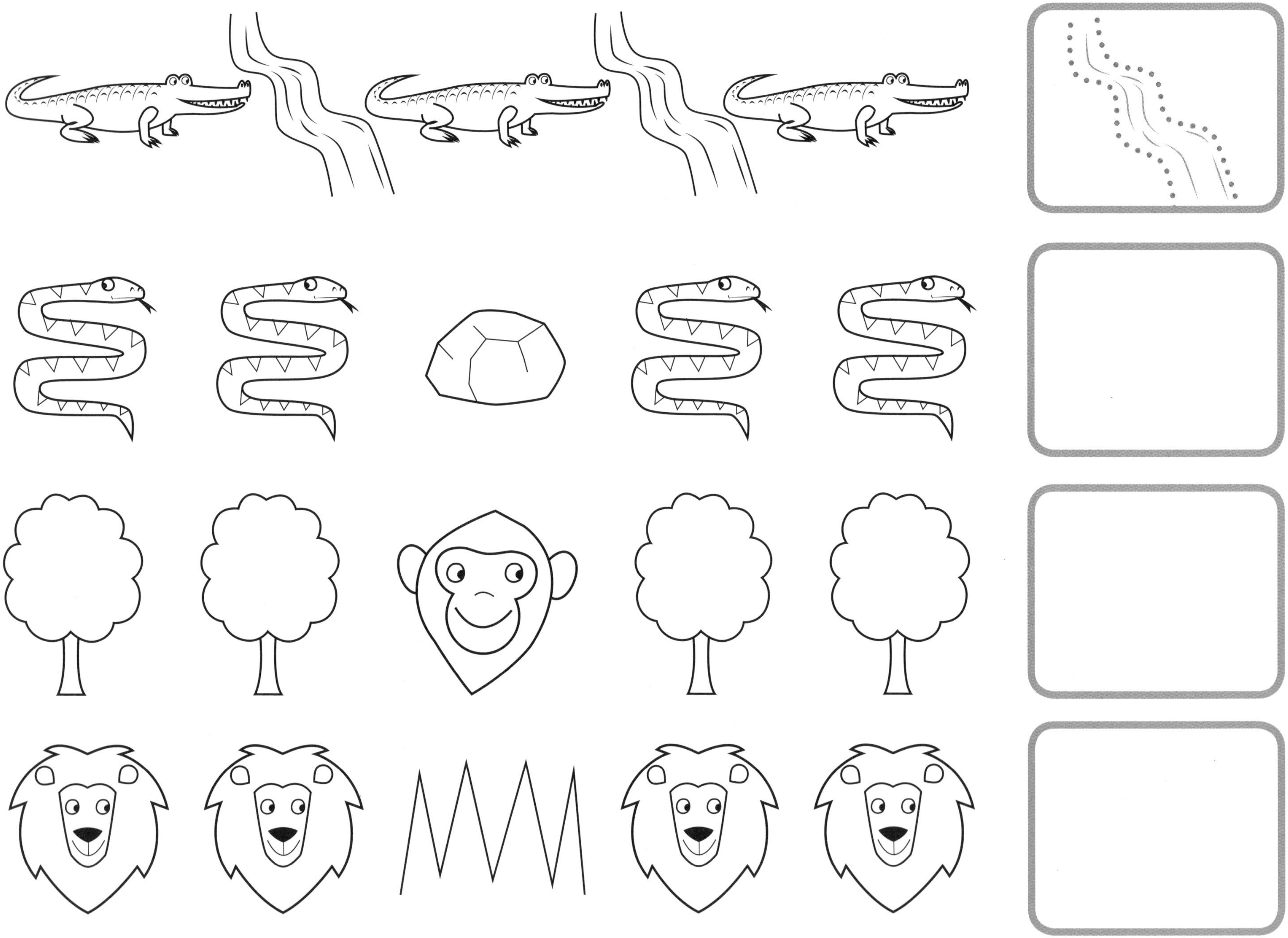

Draw yourself. Circle your favorite animal. Color.

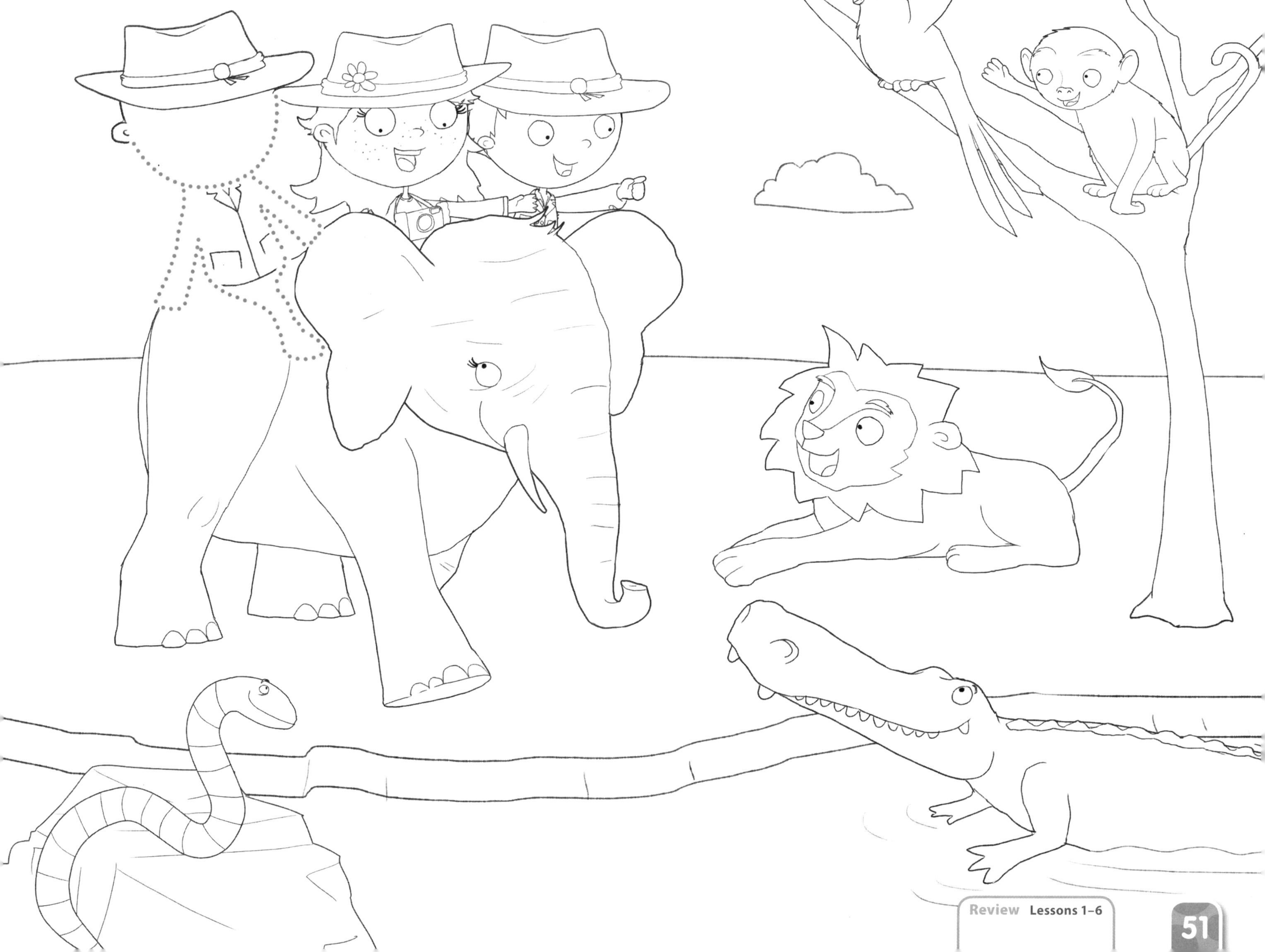

Count and write the number. Match.

8

eating

walking

running

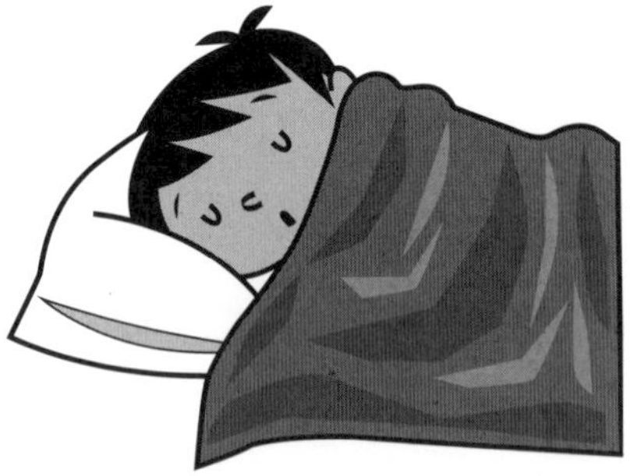

sleeping

Read and match.

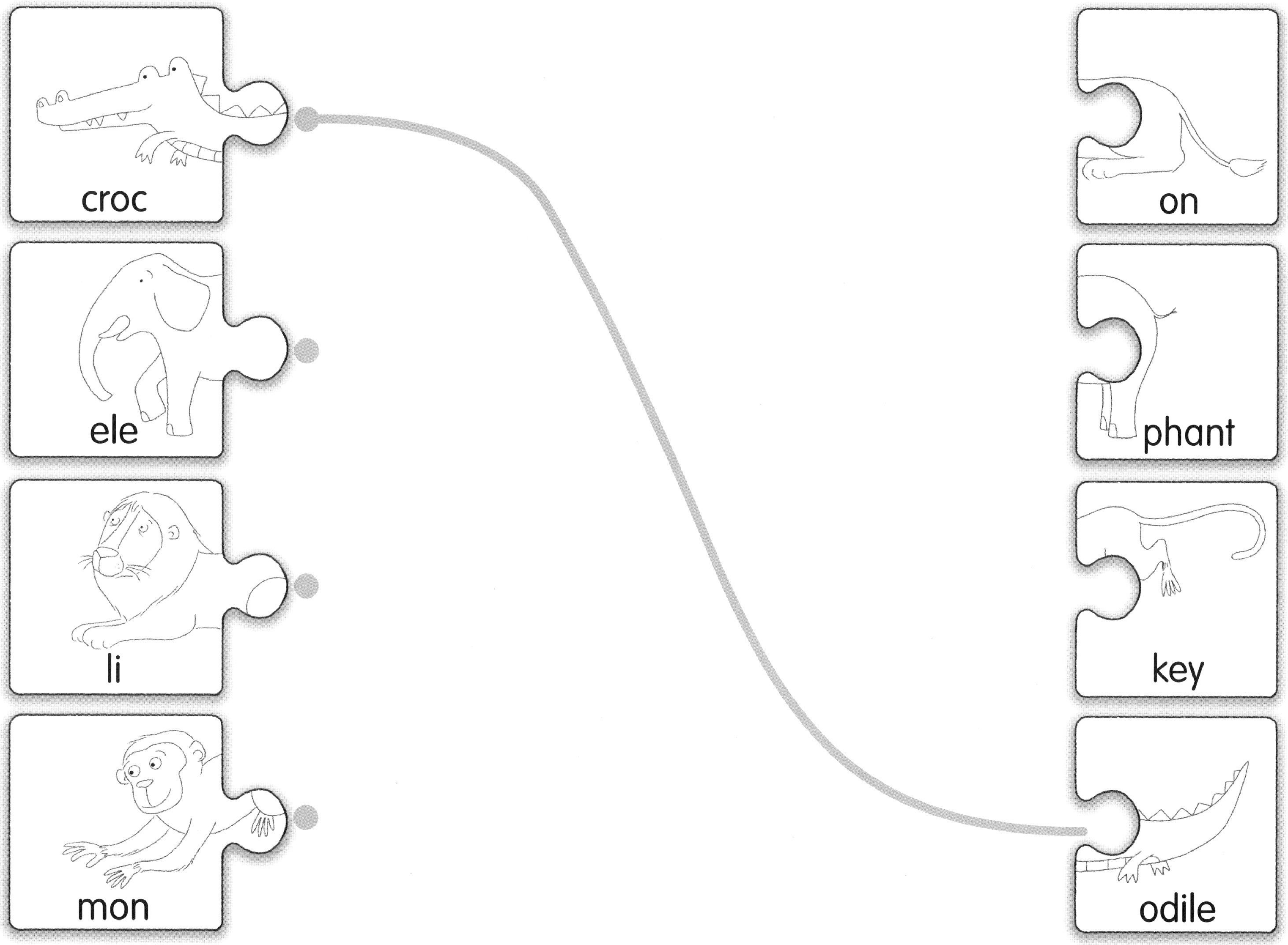
croc
ele
li
mon
on
phant
key
odile

Connect the dots. Color.

1
2
3
4
5
6
7
8
9
10
11
12
13
14
15
16
17
18

Numeracy **New numbers:** 17 and 18
Ordering numbers (1–18)

Trace and match.

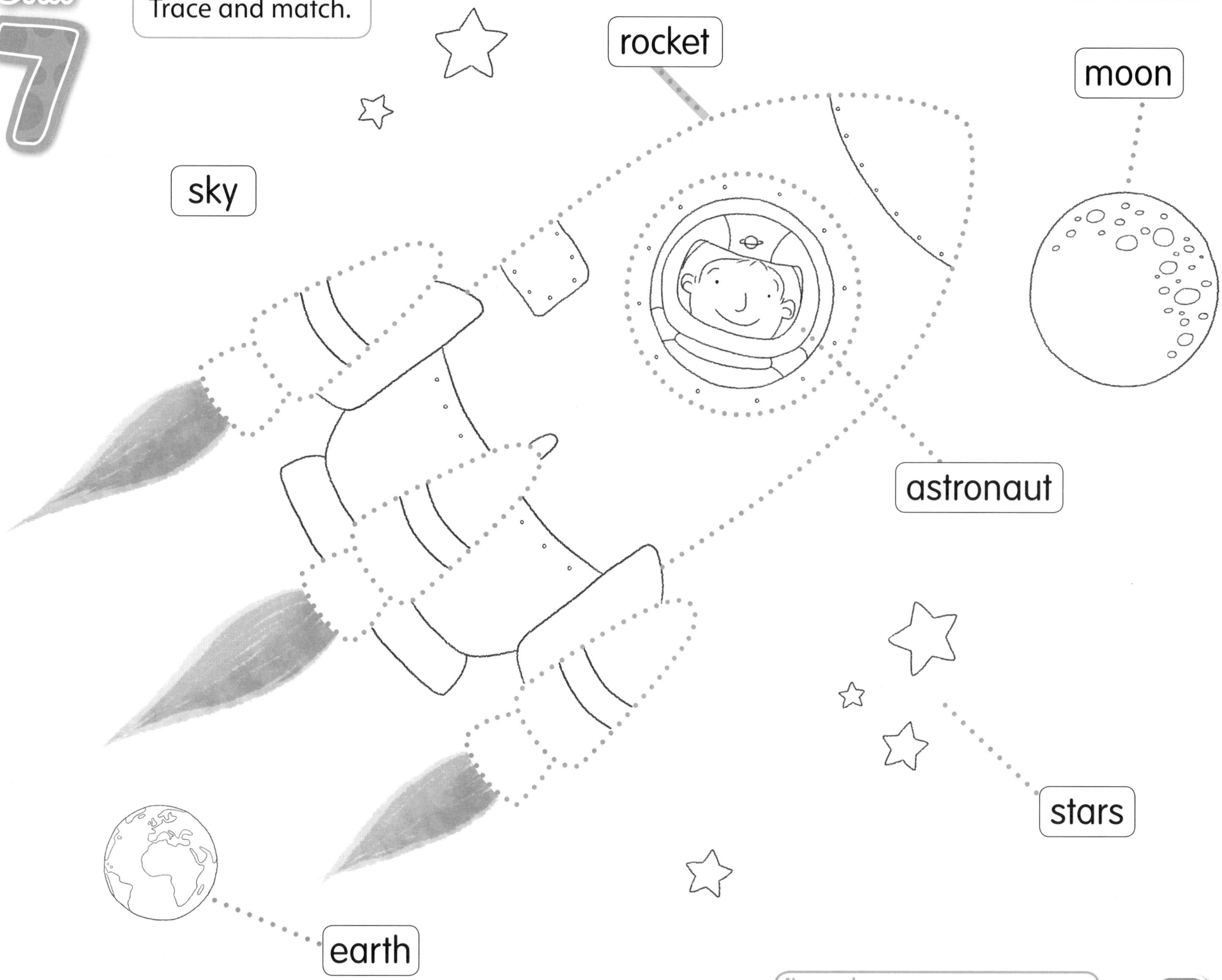
rocket
moon
sky
astronaut
stars
earth

New words
Vocabulary: *astronaut, rocket, earth, sky, stars, moon*

Who's in the story? Look and ✔ or ✘.

Little Star ☑

Robot ☐

Daisy ☐

Mouse ☐

Robin ☐

Monster ☐

Draw the path. Say *Let's go to the …*

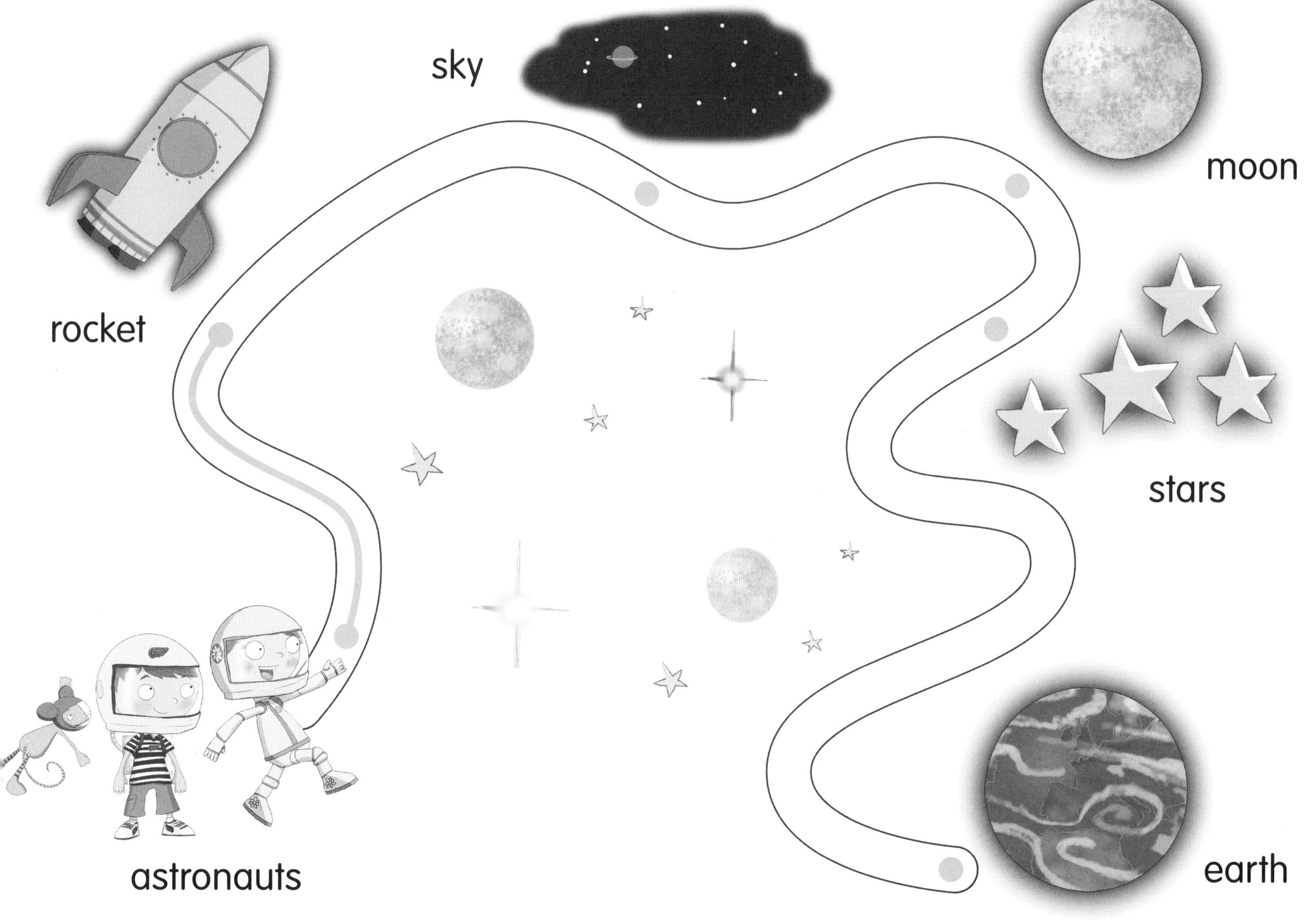
sky
moon
rocket
stars
astronauts
earth

Look and match.

1

2

3

4

daytime

nighttime

5

6

7

8

Smart topic **Daytime and nighttime**
Vocabulary: *daytime, sun, nighttime*

Look and circle 6 differences in Picture 2.

Connect the dots and color.

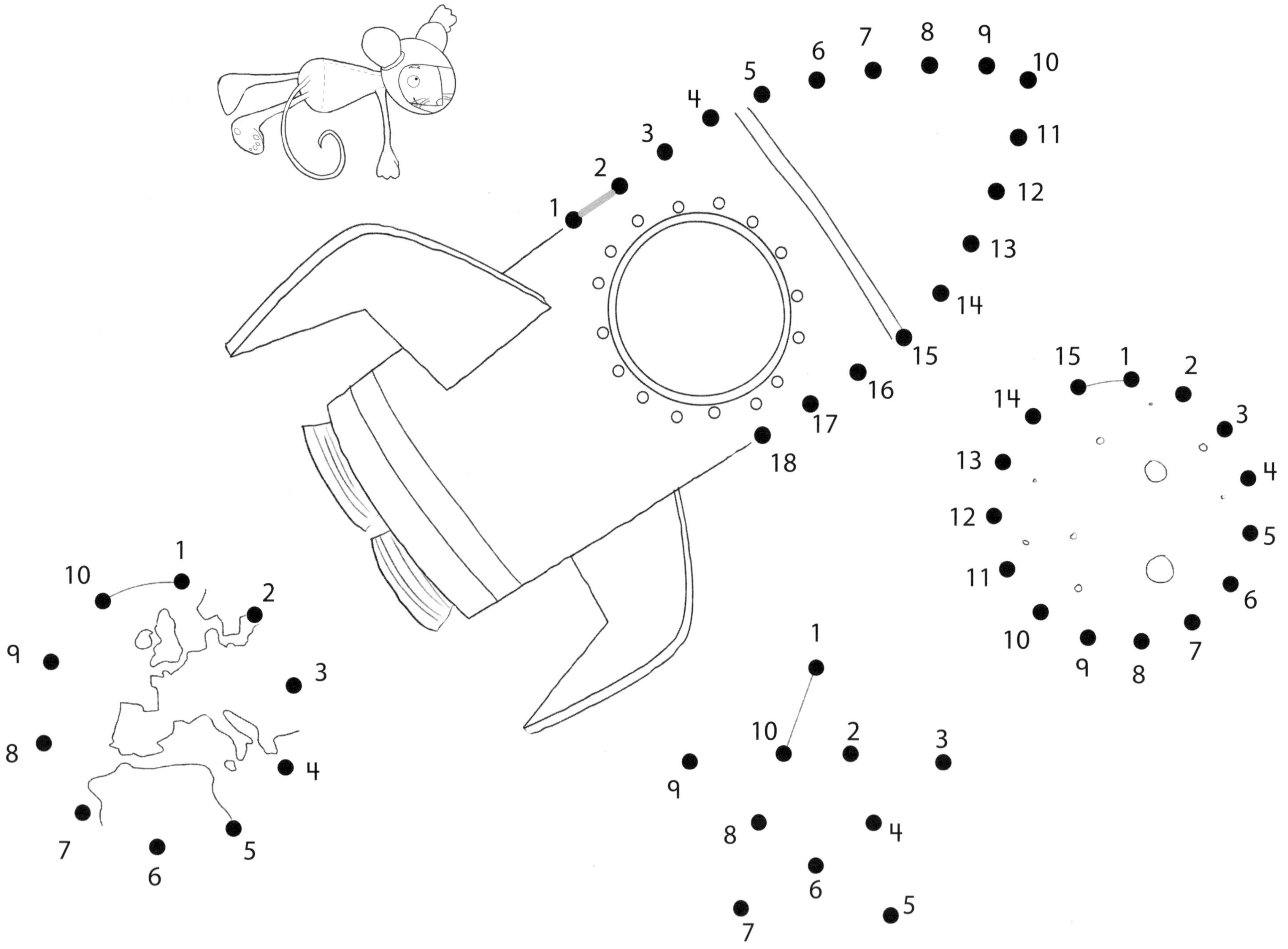

Trace, draw, and color.

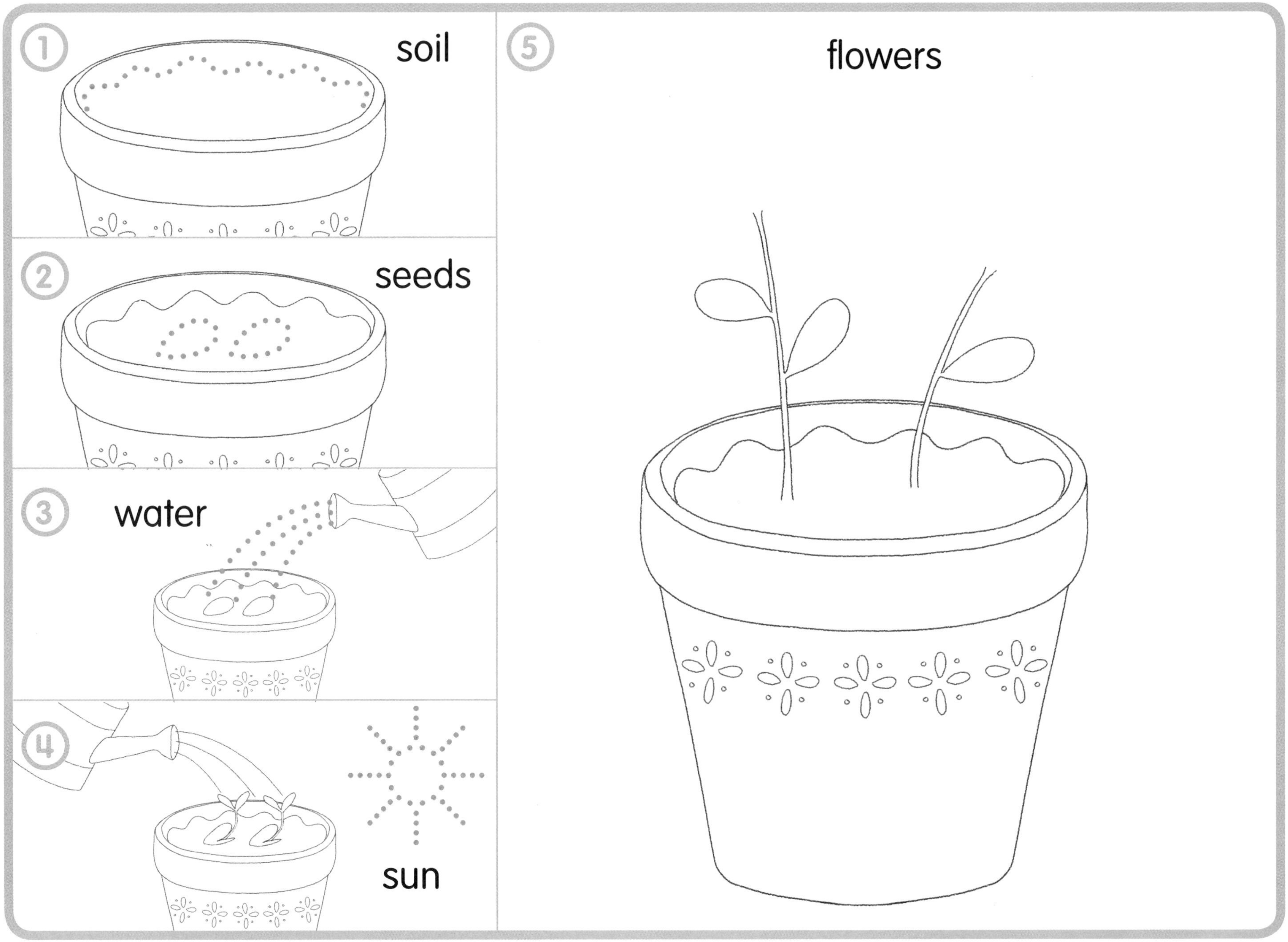
1
soil
2
seeds
3
water
4
sun
5
flowers

Read, trace, and circle.

Flowers need …

seeds		
soil		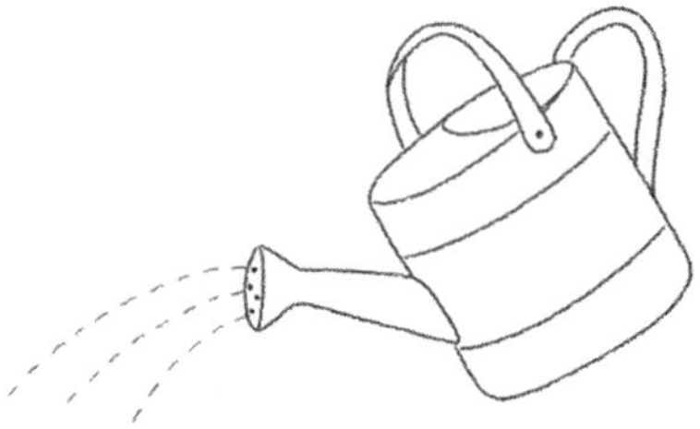
water		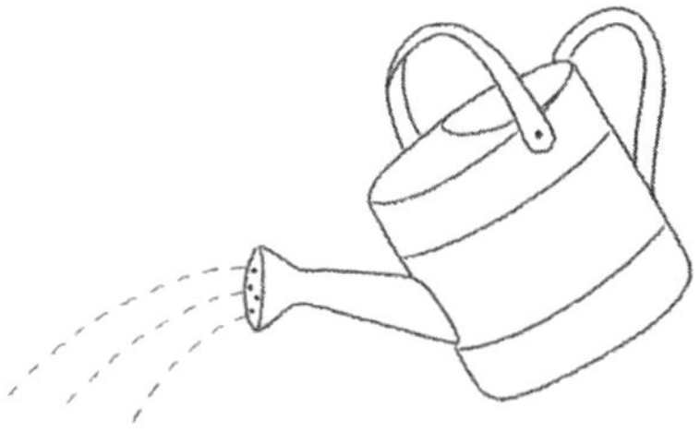
sun		

Literacy Word recognition; tracing whole words
Vocabulary: *water, soil, sun, seeds*

Write the next number.

16	17	12		10	
11		8		15	
19		13		9	
14		18		17	

Read and color. Trace and match.

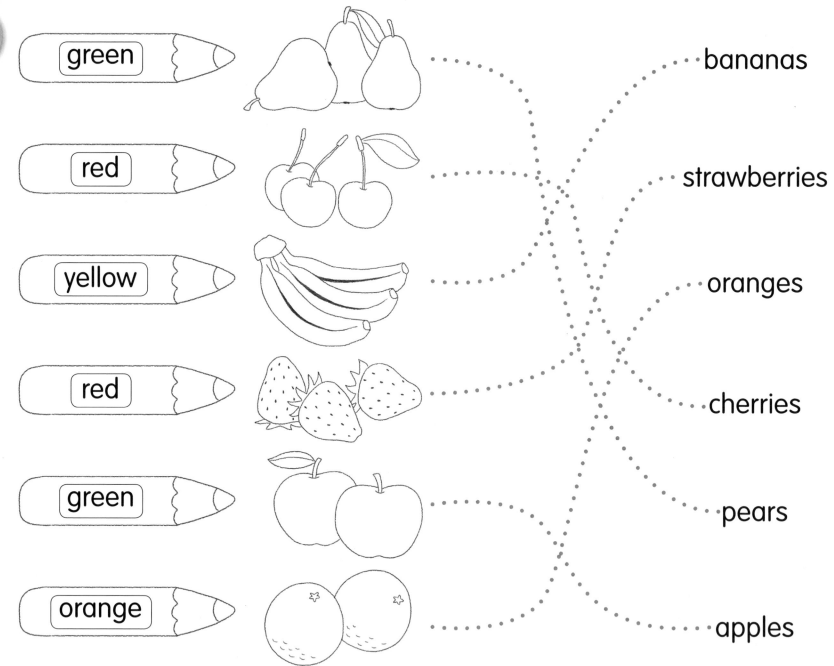

green	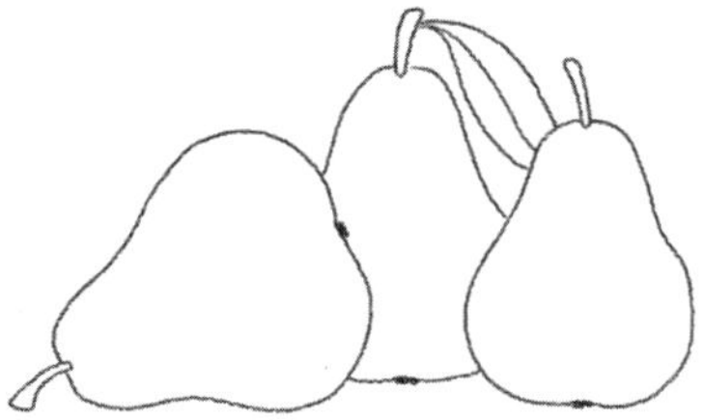	bananas
red		strawberries
yellow	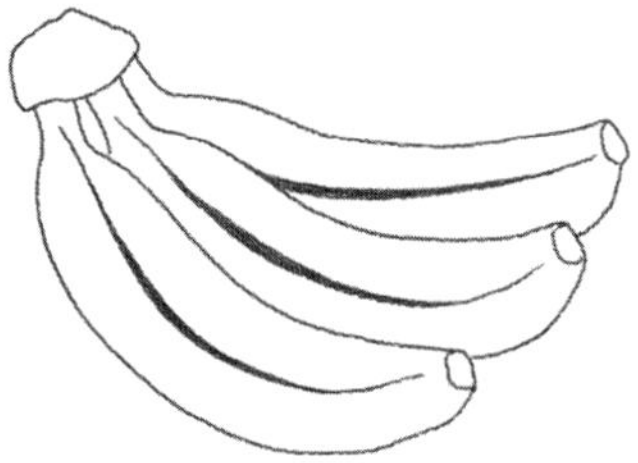	oranges
red		cherries
green		pears
orange	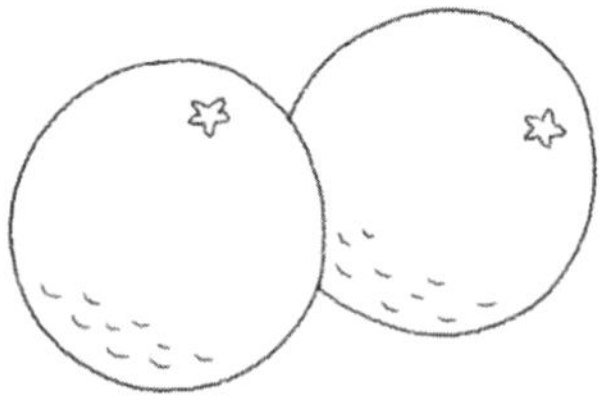	apples

New words
Vocabulary: *apples, pears, oranges, bananas, cherries, strawberries*

Trace, count, write, and match.

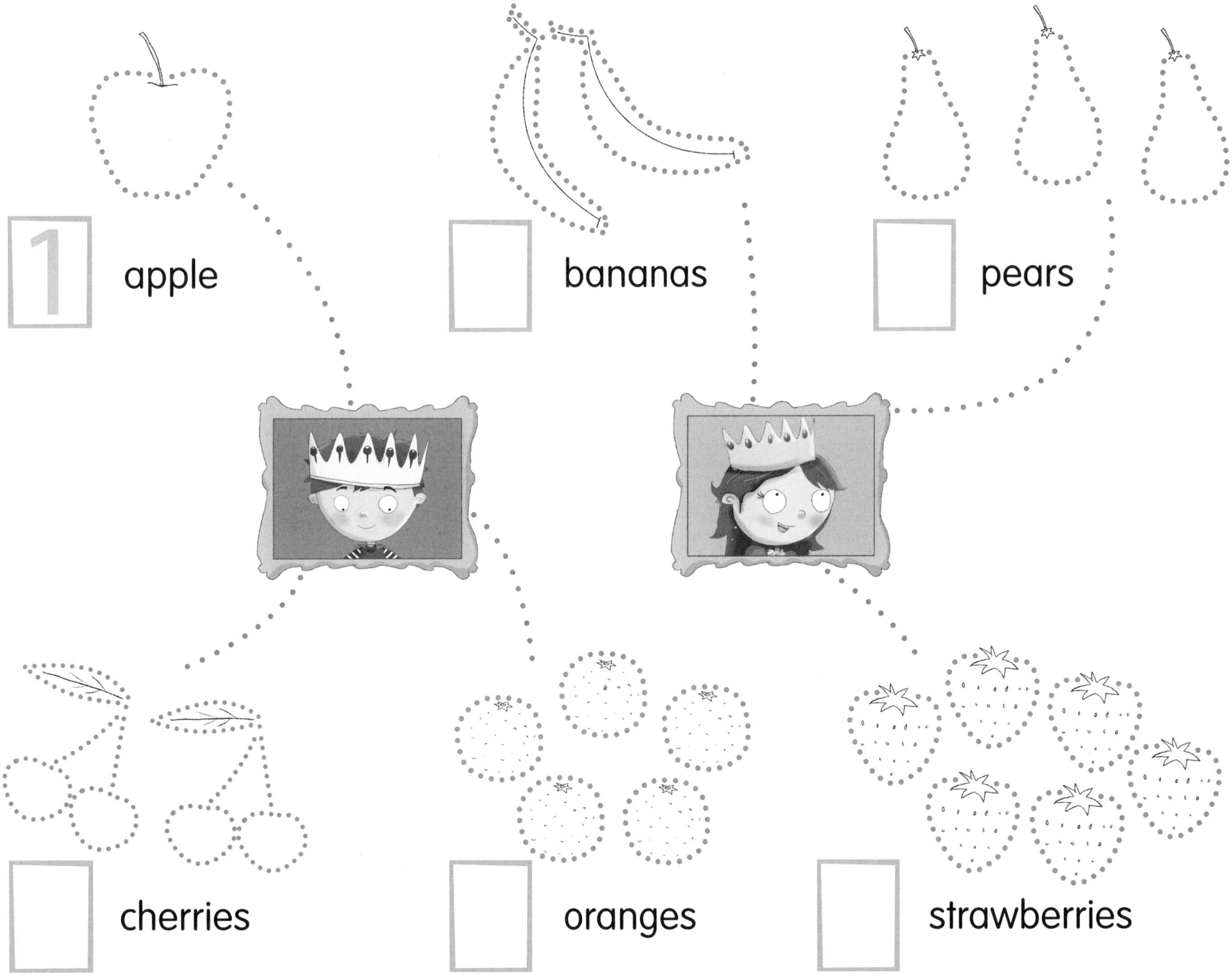
1 apple
bananas
pears
cherries
oranges
strawberries

Read and ✔. Say *I like apples.*

1

apples ☑

pears ☐

2

cherries ☐

strawberries ☐

3

bananas ☐

cherries ☐

4

pears ☐

apples ☐

5

oranges ☐

strawberries ☐

6

oranges ☐

bananas ☐

Match and color.

thirsty
hungry

Read and color.

1 red
2 yellow
3 green
4 orange
5 blue
6 black
7 white
8 pink

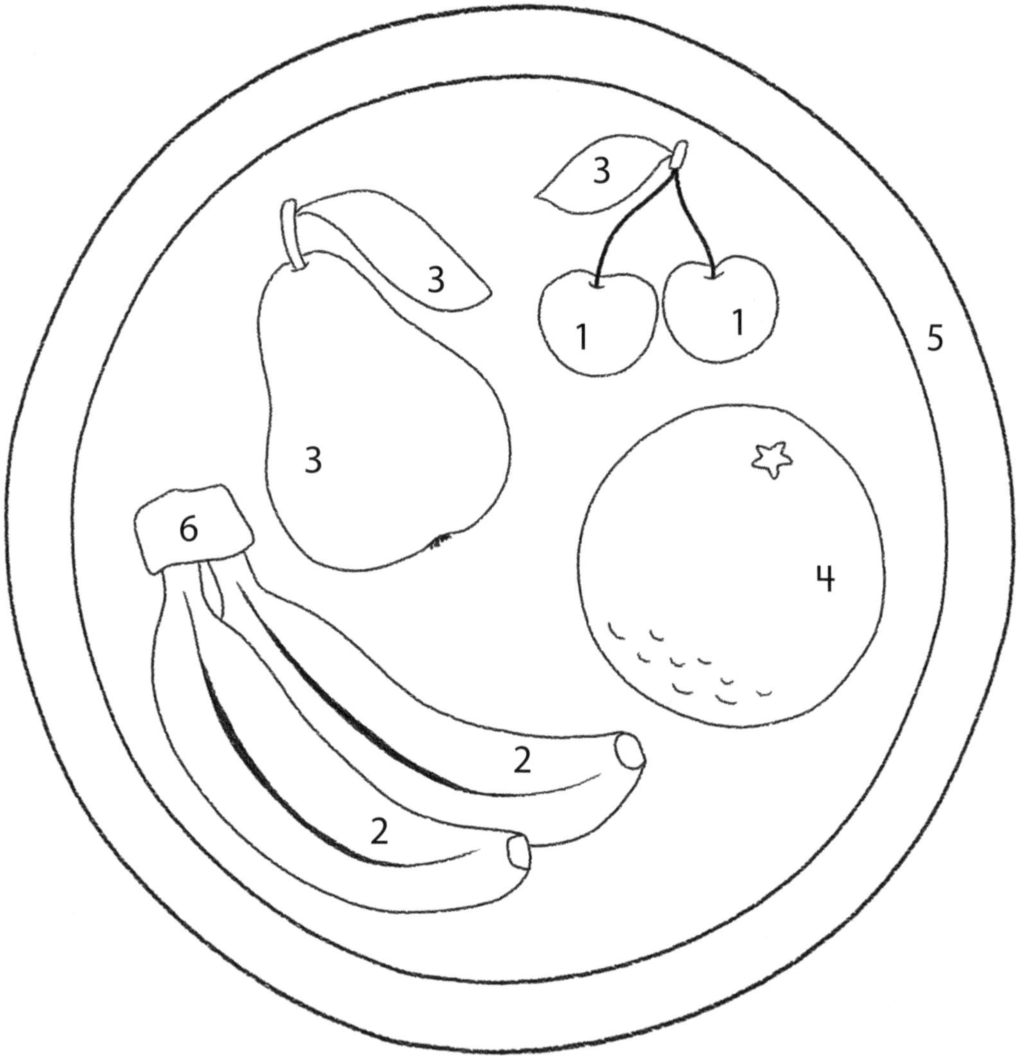
3
3
1
1
5
3
4
6
2
2

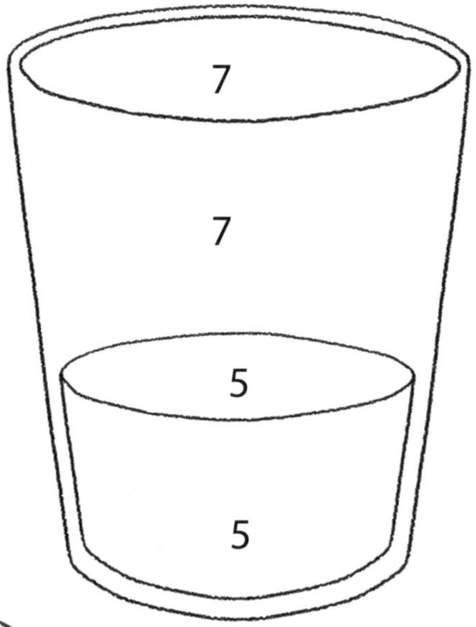
7
7
5
5

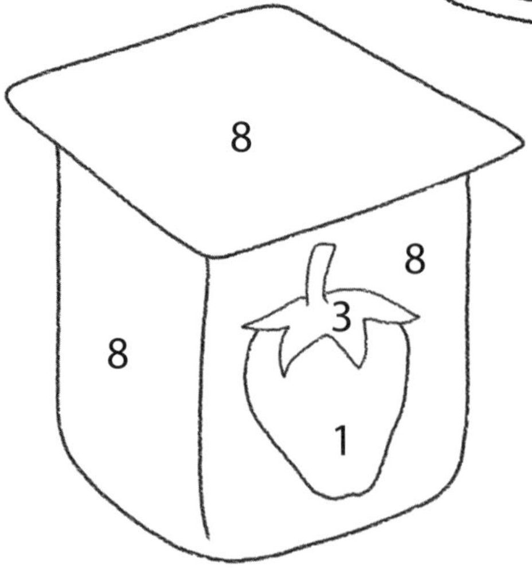
8
8
3
8
1

What's in your lunchbox? Draw and color.

Look and draw.

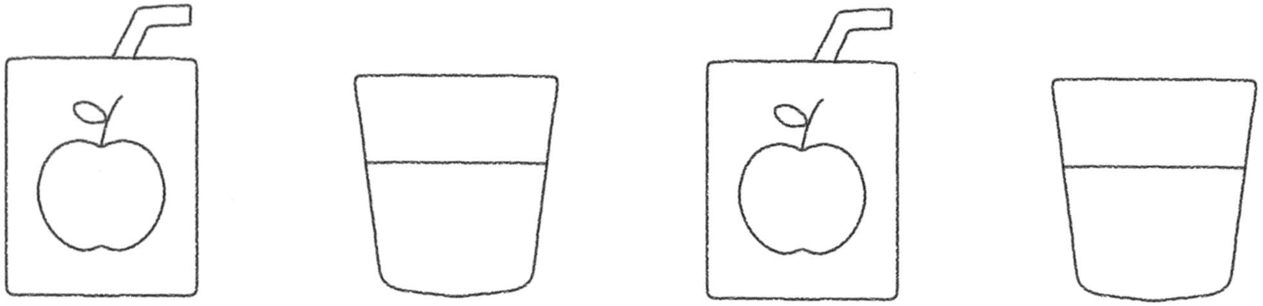

juice milk

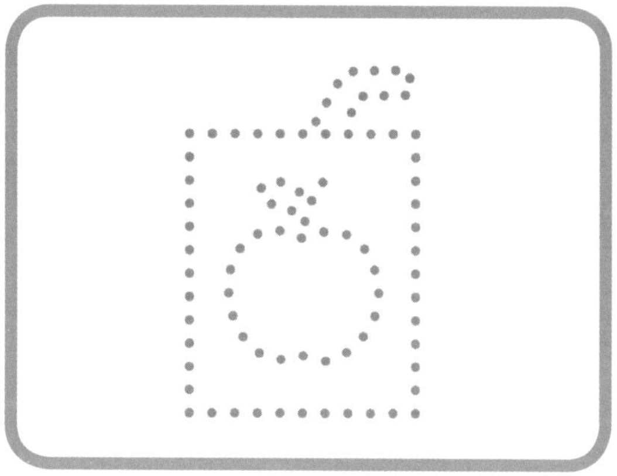

water

Read, trace, and circle.

I'm ...

hungry		
thirsty		
hungry		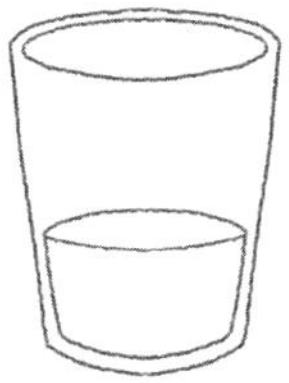
thirsty	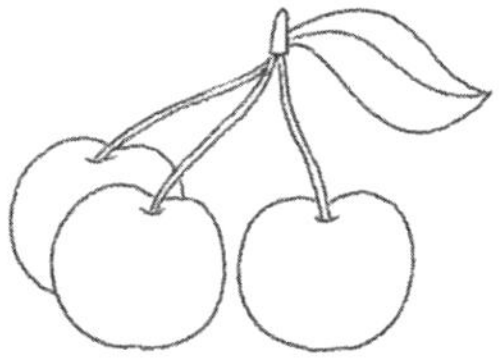	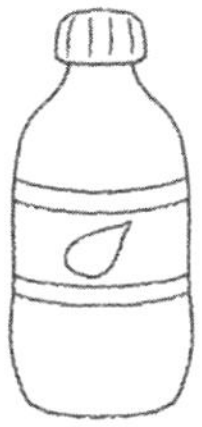

Literacy Word recognition; tracing whole words
Vocabulary: *hungry, thirsty*

Count, write, and circle.

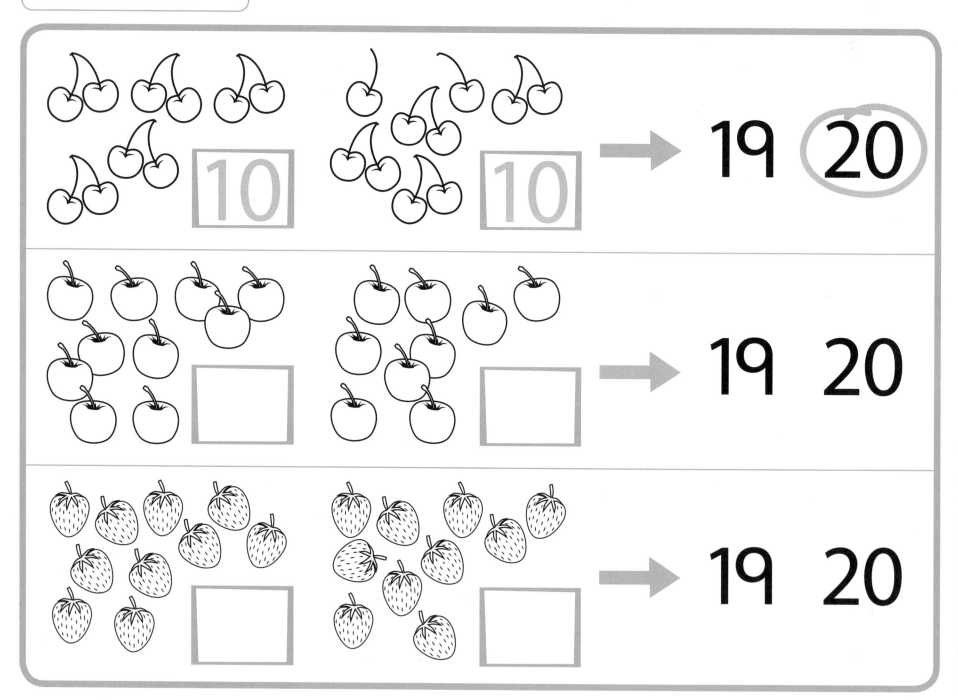

10

10

→ 19 20

→ 19 20

→ 19 20